LISTEN TO THE LOON

LISTEN TO THE LOON

An Intermediate Listening Program

Joan Roberta White

OXFORD

Oxford University Press
70 Wynford Drive, Don Mills, Ontario M3C 1J9

Oxford New York
Athens Auckland Bangkok Bombay
Calcutta Cape Town Dar es Salaam Delhi
Florence Hong Kong Istanbul Karachi
Kuala Lumpur Madras Madrid Melbourne
Mexico City Nairobi Paris Singapore
Taipei Tokyo Toronto

and associated companies in
Berlin Ibadan

Oxford is a trademark of Oxford University Press

This book is printed on permanent (acid-free) paper.

Page 87 Robert Service. Extracts from 'The Cremation of Sam McGee,' and 'The Shooting of Dan McGrew' from *Collected Poems of Robert Service*, McGraw-Hill Ryerson, 1971. Reprinted courtesy of the Estate of Robert Service.

CANADIAN CATALOGUING IN PUBLICATION DATA
White, Joan Roberta, 1943-
    Listen to the Loon : an intermediate listening program : student book

Includes bibliographical references.
ISBN 0-19-541175-7

1. English language - Textbooks for second language learners.★ 2. Listening. I. Title.

PE1128.W487 1997   428.3'4   C96-931960-6

Managing Editor: Monica Schwalbe
Copyeditors: Jill Bryant, Irene Cox
Cover illustration: Caroline Price
Cover and interior design: Brett Miller
Page composition: Heather Delfino
Photo research: Patricia Buckley Editorial Services
Illustrations: Paul Sneath of free&Creative

Printed and bound in Canada
1 2 3 4   97 98 99 00

Contents

• •

Acknowledgements

Thank you to the following students who contributed recipes to my unit on Manitoba: Inna Nei, Magda Sekaly, Lulit Woldu, and Rosalinda Arnoni.

Thanks to Martha Flaherty, an Inuit friend, who helped me with the unit on Nunavut. Her translation of my introduction of the unit is in Inuktitut (syllabary and orthography).

Thank you to Marguerite Hum for helping with the read-through of my final manuscript.

Finally, I would like to thank Robert Doyle for his confidence in my manuscript and his enthusiasm for the project.

About the Author

Joan White has been involved in teaching all levels of adult ESL since 1985 for Ontario's Carleton Board of Education. At present, she is developing a program for teaching ESL through computers. She has a TESL Certificate from the Ministry of Citizenship and Culture, a Level II Ontario Teacher's Certificate, and a Certificate for Teachers of Canadian Citizenship. She has been a presenter and facilitator at several TESL conferences and workshops, and is the author of *Half Hour Helper* and *Advanced Half Hour Helper,* two puzzle and activity books for teachers and learners of ESL. She has also been doing research and writing projects for the educational division at the National Museum of Nature in Ottawa.

About This Book

• •

Listen to the Loon is a listening activity program with a difference. Intermediate to advanced students will enjoy the challenge of developing their listening proficiency while learning about Canada.

The program includes a cassette, *Student Book*, and *Teacher's Book*. Short talks on the cassette present a special feature of each province and territory of Canada, including Nunavut. The final talk describes the country as a whole. The *Student Book* provides introductions, photos, and a variety of activities as outlined below.

Each unit in the *Student Book* is divided into the following parts.

INTRODUCTION

A short introduction and photograph give the students an idea of what the talk on the tape will be about. There are suggestions in the *Teacher's Book* for additional information or activities to prepare students for the talk.

VOCABULARY PREVIEW

Five to seven words or phrases found in the talk are presented. Students write down what they think the words or phrases mean. They can work with a partner or use a dictionary to complete this task.

SENTENCE CLUES

In this section, a dictation exercise consisting of three to five sentences provides a further vocabulary preview. The first three sentences are a cloze exercise and the last two are straight dictation. The Sentence Clues are on the cassette and are transcribed in the *Teacher's Book*.

LISTENING TO THE TALK

The talk is presented on the cassette. Students listen once for the main idea. As students listen a second time, they take notes using the Listening Chart in the *Student Book*. Some students may need to listen multiple times to get all the details. As a variation, students could work in pairs or small groups to share the listening task.

COMPREHENSION

In this section, students do one of several types of comprehension activities to reinforce the presentation in the talk:

- Answering Questions
- Completing Cloze Exercises

- Identifying True and False Statements
- Unscrambling Words
- Joining Split Sentences
- Unscrambling Sentences
- Putting Sentences in Order

In some cases, students are asked to listen to the talk again as they do the exercise to find the answers. In other instances, they work from memory and can check their answers afterwards by listening to the talk again.

VOCABULARY EXPANSION

Vocabulary from the talk is developed through a variety of exercises including:

- Antonyms, Synonyms, or Homonyms
- Comparatives
- Compound Words
- Idioms
- Word Forms
- Word Meanings
- Passive Verbs and Pronoun Relationships

FOLLOW UP

There are several different types of follow-up activities. All types are not necessarily presented in each unit. Teachers can choose among these activities according to the interests and needs of their students.

- *Talking* Using the notes in their Listening Charts and answers to the Comprehension sections, students prepare their own talks about the subject and present them to another student, group, or class.

- *Researching* Students do a research project relevant to the talk. This research could involve additional information about the subject or an exercise to contrast and compare the information in the talk with something similar in their country of origin.

- *Writing* Students prepare a writing assignment following the talk about:

  - the characters in the talk
  - what happened before or after the event in the talk
  - a similar experience the students have had
  - a similar person, place, or thing in the students' countries of origin
  - a description of a process that follows the form used in the talk

• *Interviewing* Students interview someone on a subject related to the talk. Students might find it most convenient to telephone someone for an interview. Alternatively, teachers could arrange for a guest speaker, for whom the students would prepare a set of interview questions. Another option is to have students role play an interview using information from their Listening Charts and Comprehension exercises.

• *Making or Labelling a Diagram and Filling in a Chart* Students are asked to label a diagram, fill in a chart, or create a picture related to the information in the talk.

• *Describing a Process* Students work in pairs or small groups to read out and follow recipes, to compare Canadian recipes with those from their cultures, to describe foods and how to prepare them, or to match sentences describing a process with pictures.

• *Taking a Field Trip* Students could visit museums or other sites related to the talks and report back on their experiences.

• *Filling in a Time Line* Students are asked to relate events to a time line. Answers are in the *Teacher's Book*.

British Columbia

Canada's Rain Forests

• •

INTRODUCTION

If you hear the term *rain forest*, you naturally think of the hot and humid jungles of South America. Did you know that we have rain forests in Canada? They are on the west coast in the province of British Columbia. Rain forests do not have to be in hot climates. A rain forest is made up of big trees growing closely together in a damp area, along with lots of mosses and ferns.

VOCABULARY PREVIEW

Write the meanings of the following words. You may use a dictionary if you need one.

1. coast (noun) _____

2. temperate (adjective)_____

3. tropical (adjective) _____

4. minerals (noun) _____

5. current (noun) _____

6. reserves (noun) _____

 ### SENTENCE CLUES

Listen carefully to the following sentences and fill in the blanks.

1. The area along the _____ of B.C. has a very _____ climate.

2. On the other hand, the climate in Central America is quite _____.

3. Canada is a country _____.

4. In some places, _____.

LISTENING TO THE TALK

You will hear a talk about the temperate rain forests of British Columbia. It will explain why Canada has rain forests and where in the province you can see them.

The first time you hear the tape, just listen for the main ideas. As you listen for a second time, make notes using this chart. Fill in the correct number in the right-hand column.

Listening Chart: Canada's Rain Forests

Fact	Number
Height of big trees in most parts of the world	
Height of tall trees in tropical rain forests of South America	
Height of trees in Canada's rain forests	
Years that loggers destroyed a lot of trees on the west coast	
Age of some trees in Stanley Park in Vancouver	
Age of some trees in Cathedral Grove Park on Vancouver Island	
Number of years ago that fire destroyed much of the rain forest on Vancouver Island	

 COMPREHENSION

After listening to the talk on the tape and filling in your listening chart, do the following exercise. Listen as many times as necessary to find the answers.

Split Sentences

The beginnings and endings of sentences are printed on the next page. Find the correct ending for each sentence beginning. Write the end of the sentence in the blank.

Beginnings

1. In our rain forests, the trees _____.

2. Trees on the coast grow so tall because _____

_____.

3. The weather is warmer along the west coast for a longer time because _____

_____.

4. During the 1800s and early 1900s, a lot of these beautiful giant trees _____.

5. Now some areas of rain forest can continue to survive because _____

_____.

6. Many parks and reserves in British Columbia _____

_____.

7. The grandest rain forest park in Canada _____.

8. The trees in Cathedral Grove _____.

Endings

a) have fascinating examples of the beautiful, giant trees.

b) are either 800 years old or 300 years old.

c) of the warm winds and currents from the Pacific Ocean.

d) they are protected by the government.

e) they have the right amounts of sunlight, warm temperatures, and water.

f) can reach almost 70 metres.

g) were destroyed by loggers.

h) is Cathedral Grove on Vancouver Island.

Root	Superlative	Opposite Root	Opposite Superlative
high	highest	low	lowest
	tallest		
	wettest		
	youngest		
	warmest		
	biggest		
	longest		
	thickest		
	oldest		

VOCABULARY EXPANSION

Antonyms

Fill in the chart of adjectives above. The superlative form is given. Determine the root word first and then write its opposite in the appropriate box, followed by the opposite word's superlative form. The first one has been done for you.

Idioms

Here are some idioms involving rain and trees.

Idiom	Meaning
a) *it never rains, but it pours*	when one thing goes wrong, so do others
b) *come rain or shine*	whatever the weather

Idiom	Meaning
c) *to rain cats and dogs*	to rain heavily
d) *money doesn't grow on trees*	you don't get money for nothing
e) *you can't see the forest for the trees*	you don't have a clear understanding of the whole because you are looking at only a small aspect

Which idiom would you use in each of the following sentences?

1. "I'm sorry son," explained Mr. Braun, "you can't have that new computer! _____

    _____, you know."

2. We're going on a trip into the rain forest tomorrow, _____.

3. Poor Mamoud! He had a minor accident a block from work. He forgot his wallet at home.

    The police were a long time arriving at the scene. The other driver left before they

    came. Now Mamoud is late for work. _____.

4. The situation in that small European country is so complicated that all the politicians involved

    _____.

5. We are planning to go on a picnic at the beach today, but if _____,

    we'll have to stay home.

FOLLOW UP

Talking

Using your listening chart and the answers to your Comprehension section to help you, tell another group or class about the rain forests in B.C.

Researching

Look for more information about B.C.'s rain forests and for information about a *tropical* rain forest. Compare and contrast these two types of rain forests by looking at average temperature, latitude in the world, nearby water, height of trees, age of trees, and types of trees.

Interviewing

- If possible, interview someone who has visited a B.C. rain forest.
- If you happen to live in the Vancouver or Victoria area, go on a class visit to one of the parks described in the talk.
- Alternatively, use the information in this unit to role play an interview with a rain-forest expert.

Labelling a Diagram

Label the following diagram. Use these words.

branch   leaves   needles   roots   trunk

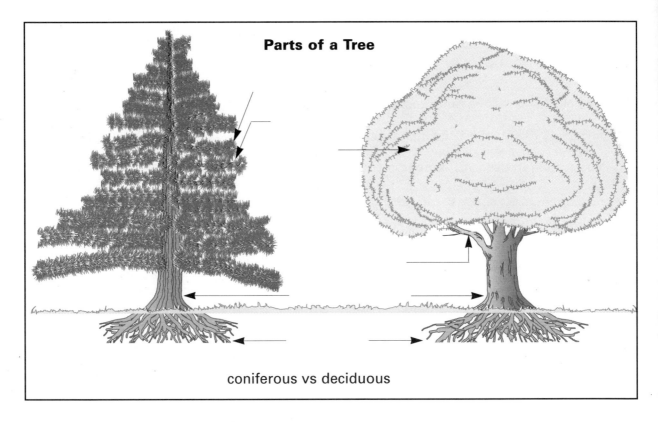

Parts of a Tree

coniferous vs deciduous

❖ More than one-third of all Canada's land mass is covered with trees — that's 906 million hectares!

❖ There are nine different forest regions.

❖ There are 140 different kinds of trees.

Unit Two

Alberta

Banff National Park

• •

INTRODUCTION

Canada has 34 national parks and reserves. The purpose of the parks is to protect the natural resources and animals of the country. The parks are for the education and enjoyment of the nation. They are found in all areas of the country, from the Pacific Ocean to the Atlantic Ocean and from north of the Arctic Circle to the southern-most point in Canada. You will hear about our oldest national park, Banff National Park, in Alberta.

VOCABULARY PREVIEW

Write the meanings of the following words. Use a dictionary if you need one.

1. national (adjective) _____

2. alpine (adjective) _____

3. glacier (noun) _____

4. sulphur (noun/adjective) _____

5. gaze (verb) _____

6. majestic (adjective) _____

 ### SENTENCE CLUES

Listen carefully to the following sentences and fill in the blanks.

1. Canada's _____ anthem is 'O Canada.'

2. Small _____ flowers bloom brightly in the tundra areas.

3. Icefields and _____ provide life by giving water to many areas of the park.

4. Go for a swim in the _____.

5. _____?

LISTENING TO THE TALK

You will now hear the talk about our first national park. The first time you hear the tape, just listen for the main ideas. As you listen for a second time, make notes using the following chart.

Listening Chart: Banff National Park

Year the park was established	
Year the park was renamed	
Population of Banff	
Number of visitors per year	
Recreational activities 1. ___ 2. ___ 3. ___ 4. ___ 5. ___ 6. ___	

 COMPREHENSION

Answering Questions

Answer the following questions after listening to the talk on the tape and filling in the chart above. Listen as many times as necessary to find the answers.

1. When was our oldest national park established?

___

2. When was the park named Banff National Park?

___

3. Who was responsible for its creation?

_____

4. Why are the lakes in the park so cold?

_____

5. Where is one place you can go downhill skiing in the park?

_____

6. Where is the only 'hot spot' in the park?

_____

7. How many people live in the town of Banff?

_____

8. What mountains are part of Banff National Park?

_____

9. What can adventurous campers do in the park?

_____

10. Why is Banff National Park so famous?

_____

VOCABULARY EXPANSION

Compound Words

Match a word from Column A with a word from Column B to make a compound word you heard in the talk.

Column A	Column B
backpacking_____	shoeing
mountain_____	hill
sun_____	fields
down_____	top
wonder_____	shine
ice_____	ground
cross-_____	country
snow_____	land
camp_____	packing

Antonyms

Part 1

The following words are in the talk you heard. Work with a partner and find a word that has the opposite meaning. If you want help, use a dictionary or a thesaurus.

1. western ≠ _____

2. majestic ≠ _____

3. established ≠ _____

4. fascinating ≠ _____

5. deep ≠ _____

6. high ≠ _____

Part 2

Now use the new words to fill in the blanks in the following sentences. They won't appear in the same order as above!

a) The professor's lecture was quite _____.

b) The Maritimes are in _____ Canada.

c) Compared with kings and queens, most people lead very _____ lives.

d) Many wildlife areas are being _____ by the development of businesses and housing.

e) After a rain, _____ puddles disappear quickly.

f) The _____ tides in Fundy National Park reveal many fascinating sights!

Comparatives

Some comparative words are formed simply by adding *er* or *est*. Sometimes you have to double the final consonant before adding the ending. Other comparatives are formed by using the words *more* or *most* in front of the adjective. Fill in the chart on the next page with the proper words.

Adjective	Comparative	Superlative
famous		
old		
small		
deep		
magnificent		
exciting		
hot		
steamy		
high		
adventurous		

FOLLOW UP

Guess Where?

In which province or territory do you think the following parks are located? The geographical location or the language might give you a clue. You can refer to an atlas if you need help.

1. Auyuittuq _____

2. Cape Breton Highlands _____

3. Fundy _____

4. Grasslands _____

5. La Mauricie _____

6. Pacific Rim _____

7. Prince Albert _____

8. St. Lawrence Islands _____

9. Terra Nova _____

10. Wood Buffalo _____

Researching

Do some research to find information about one of the parks listed on the previous page or another national park or reserve. Include where the park is located, the features of the natural environment, the wildlife, and recreational activities in the park.

Talking

Using your listening chart and the answers to your Comprehension section to help you, tell another group or class about Banff National Park. Or, present the information you found while researching another national park.

❖ Wood Buffalo National Park is the largest park in the world — 44 800 square kilometres! It's partly in northern Alberta and partly in the Northwest Territories.

Canadian Dinosaurs

INTRODUCTION

Scientists believe that millions of years ago Canada was very different from what it's like today. Much of the land in western Canada was tropical forest and there was a large inland sea. The weather was hot and humid all the time. Human beings had not appeared on the earth. The earth was ruled by dinosaurs. Then, 65 million years ago, the dinosaurs disappeared.

VOCABULARY PREVIEW

Write the meanings of the following words. Use a dictionary if you need help.

1. fossil (noun) _____

2. tropical (adjective) _____

3. reptile (noun) _____

4. creature (noun) _____

5. limbs (noun) _____

6. vicious (adjective) _____

7. talon (noun) _____

SENTENCE CLUES

Listen carefully to the following sentences and fill in the blanks.

1. The only way we know dinosaurs lived is because we have found _____.

2. Many _____ live in _____ countries.

3. Development by humans is taking away the natural homes of many wild _____.

4. Many animals _____.

5. _____.

LISTENING TO THE TALK

Listen to the talk and you will hear about the dinosaurs that lived in what is now Alberta, Canada. The first time you hear the tape, just listen for the main ideas. As you listen for a second time, make notes using the following chart.

Listening Chart: Canadian Dinosaurs

Location of Dinosaur Provincial Park		
When dinosaurs lived		
Size and weight of smaller varieties		
Size and weight of larger varieties		
What meat eaters ate		
What vegetarians ate		
Two of these types were the smaller meat eaters. Circle them.	Tyrannosaurus Rex Stenonychosaurus	Albertosaurus Dromaeosaurus
Two of these vegetarians were covered with armour. Circle them.	Euoplocephalus Chasmosaurus	Triceratops Edmontosaurus

 ## COMPREHENSION

Fill in the Blanks

Do the following exercise after listening to the talk on the tape. Listen as many times as necessary to find the answers. Work with a partner and use the information in your charts to help you. Fill in the words from the box at the bottom of the exercise.

1. Dinosaur Provincial Park is located in _____ Alberta.

2. This area of Alberta is called the _____.

3. Dinosaurs died _____ of years ago.

4. Scientists have found _____ of _____ all over the world.

5. Meat eaters are also called _____.

6. _____ are called vegetarians.

7. Meat eaters walked around on _____ limbs.

8. The plant eaters walked on _____ legs.

9. Tyrannosaurs had sharp _____ and _____ to attack their prey.

10. Vegetarians had sharp _____ and heavy armour to protect themselves.

11. Scientists _____ about what it was like when the dinosaurs lived on the earth.

12. No one can _____ what it was really like.

badlands	bones	carnivores	claws	fossils	four	guess	know
millions	plant eaters	southern	spines	teeth	two		

VOCABULARY EXPANSION

Synonyms

Part 1

A synonym is a word that has the same or almost the same meaning as another word. Listen to the talk again and try to find a synonym for each of the following words.

1. found (verb 'to find') _____

2. hot and humid (adjectives) _____

3. huge (adjective) _____

4. animals (noun) _____

5. different (adjective) _____

6. back (adjective) _____

7. strong (adjective) _____

8. famous (adjective) _____

Part 2

You have eight sets of synonyms. Write a sentence for each set. Use the synonym you like the best from each pair.

1. _____

2. _____

3. _____

4. _____

5. _____

6. _____

7. _____

8. _____

FOLLOW UP

Talking

Using your listening chart and the answers to the Comprehension exercise to help you, tell another group or class about dinosaurs in Canada. These questions will guide you in your planned talk.

1. What are the two main types of dinosaurs? What did they eat?

2. How long did dinosaurs live on earth?

3. When did they disappear from earth?

4. Where in Canada did they live?

5. How do we know that dinosaurs lived here?

Researching

There is a lot of information available about dinosaurs. Go to any library and you will find many books on this topic, especially in the children's section. Children love dinosaurs. If you have children, you could read some of these books to them, or maybe they will read to you. Your reading will give you some background information for the writing exercise below.

Writing

Imagine that you have entered a time machine and you have gone back in time 70 million years! You have landed on a sandbar in the area of southern Alberta. You will be staying here for 24 hours.

Look around you. What do you see? What sounds do you hear?
What have you brought with you for protection? What will you eat?
Be careful! There might be some meat eaters in the area!

Write about your experience.

Taking a Field Trip
Visit a museum. Many large museums have a dinosaur section. There are many dinosaur parks in Canada as well. Maybe there is one in your area.

* Crocodiles and alligators are descendants of the dinosaurs.
  Some people believe that dinosaurs still exist. Have you heard of Ogopogo, the sea serpent that some people believe lives in Okanagan Lake in B.C.?

Unit Three

Saskatchewan

What's in a Name?

INTRODUCTION

The province of Saskatchewan gets its name from a Cree word meaning 'swift water.' Saskatchewan is also the name of the river that runs through the city of Saskatoon. *Medicine Hat, Riga, Qu'Appelle-Moose, Minnedosa, Saskatoon,* and *Prince Albert* are all place names in Saskatchewan. Where did these names come from? Naming cities, towns, mountains, lakes, and rivers was a part of the development of the country. Was it just by chance that the capital of Saskatchewan was named *Regina*? This unit will help clear up some of the mystery.

VOCABULARY PREVIEW

Write the meanings of the following words. You may use a dictionary to help you.

1. hectare (noun) _____

2. acre (noun) _____

3. site (noun) _____

4. colony (noun) _____

5. branch (noun) _____

6. settlement (noun) _____

7. native (adjective) _____

🞀▦▦🞂 SENTENCE CLUES

Listen carefully to the following sentences and fill in the blanks.

1. One _____ equals .405 _____.

2. Early settlers often chose a _____ close to a river or a lake for their new

   _____.

3. The tree's _____.

4. _____.

🞀▦▦🞂 LISTENING TO THE TALK

You will hear a talk about how Saskatoon, Saskatchewan got its name. Your teacher will help you with the pronunciation of some of the words you will hear on the tape. The first time you hear the talk, just listen for the main ideas. As you listen for a second time, make notes using the following chart.

Listening Chart: What's in a Name?

	What important event happened?
1881	
August 18, 1882	
August 20, 1882	
1890	
1894	
1900	

COMPREHENSION

Sentence Order

Put the following sentences in the correct order by numbering them 1 through 9. Work with a partner and use your listening chart to help you.

_____   The group settled along the east side of the South Saskatchewan River.

_____   John Lake, their leader, wanted to name the new colony *Minnetonka*.

_____   Soon the railroad came west and the settlement expanded to both sides of the Saskatchewan River.

_____   The Native peoples of the area helped him change his mind.

_____   A group from Toronto bought a large area of land.

_____   Two post offices were needed to serve this growing town.

_____   The Canadian government was selling land in Saskatchewan.

_____   Some people thought the names *Saskatoon* and *Saskatchewan* were a foreign language.

_____   So he called it Saskatoon, after the berries that are native to the area.

VOCABULARY EXPANSION

Word Meanings

Many place names in Canada were derived from Native languages. There were many groups of Native peoples in Canada before the new settlers came from Europe. Some of these Native groups were Cree, Iroquois, Algonquin, Ojibwa, Chippewa, and Micmac. Most of the place names that come from Native words are spelled according to what the French and English explorers thought they heard when listening to the Native peoples talk about a place.

Can you match the names of these places with their meanings? Write the correct letter in the blank in front of each name. Don't worry if you can't answer all of them. This exercise is a challenge! Your teacher will help you with the answers.

[HINT] Their location might explain why these places were given their names. Use the index (gazetteer) in an atlas to help you find these places on a map. They could be cities, towns, lakes, rivers, or mountains. Many of the names refer to more than one place. The *Canadian Encyclopedia* is also a good resource to help you find the answers.

Examples:

Place	*Meaning*
Athabaska (Alberta)	where there are reeds
Madawaska (Ontario)	land of porcupines (Micmac)
Minnedosa (Manitoba)	swift water (Sioux)

_____ Canso	a) place where there are caribou (Inuktitut)
_____ Iqaluit	b) opposite the lofty cliff (Micmac — camsook)
_____ Malpeque	c) place of fish (Inuktitut)
_____ Ontario	d) pile of bones (Cree)
_____ Tuktuyaktok	e) large lake (Huron)
_____ Saskatchewan	f) swift water (Cree)
_____ Waskana	g) murky water (Cree)
_____ Winnipeg	h) big bay (Micmac)

FOLLOW UP

Talking

Using your listening chart and your answers to the Comprehension section, tell another group or class about how some Canadian places were named.

Researching

Try to find the source of the name of your city or town. You could also choose a lake, river, or mountain in your province or territory.

Some possible sources are the following: Native languages, important individuals in history, family names, political names, names brought from overseas.

Writing

Write a report about your research. Explain why you chose the name you did. List the people or library sources you used to gather your information.

Describing a Process

This is an easy recipe for Native Indian bread. You might enjoy making it with your class or with your family at home. Work with a partner. As he or she reads the directions, follow them step by step. Or, if you don't have access to a kitchen, dictate the directions to a partner so that you will have a copy of the recipe to take home.

How to Make *Anisk-Nah Be Pakwejigan*
(Native Indian Bread)

Method

Bring to a boil 425 mL (1 and 3/4 cups) of water.

In a bowl, mix together 150 mL (2/3 cup) white corn flour (from health food stores) and 4 mL (3/4 teaspoon) salt.

Pour the boiling water on the dry ingredients and stir until the mixture has thickened.

Stir in 125 mL (1/2 cup) of blueberries or raisins and then chill the mixture in a pan until it is set.

When it is firm, cut into slices and fry in butter.

Serve with butter or maple syrup.

DID YOU KNOW?

❖ The longest single-word place name in the world is a lake in northern Manitoba. It's called *Pekwachnamaykoskwaskwaypinwanik*. Can you pronounce it?

❖ The longest place name with more than one word is a river in New Brunswick. It's called *Lower North Branch Little Southwest Miramichi River.*

Unit Four
Manitoba

Immigrant Mosaic

• •

INTRODUCTION

All over Canada, immigrants have come to settle and bring some of their culture to their new country. The immigrant population in Manitoba is a colourful and varied blend. New Canadians have come from all over the world to add a distinctive flavour to this province.

VOCABULARY PREVIEW

Write the meanings of the following words. Use a dictionary if you need one.

1. Métis (noun) _____

2. cultivate (verb) _____

3. hectare (noun) _____

4. various (adjective) _____

5. heritage (noun) _____

SENTENCE CLUES

Listen carefully to the following sentences and fill in the blanks.

1. Louis Riel was a famous _____ who lived in Manitoba and fought for the rights of his people.

2. New immigrants had to _____ the hard-packed soil to grow crops.

3. The federal government _____

_____.

4. _____.

23

LISTENING TO THE TALK

You will hear a talk about the immigrant groups of Manitoba. You may have some things in common with these groups because you too are an immigrant in your province.

Listen to the talk twice. The first time you hear the tape, just listen for the main ideas. As you listen for a second time, make notes using the following chart.

Listening Chart: Immigrant Mosaic

	Circle the names of the people, or the country, associated with the date in the left-hand column.				
1870	American First Nations	Chinese Irish	English Japanese	French Métis	German Scots
1890	American Norway	Denmark Polish	English Russia	Iceland Sweden	
1910	Belgium Poland	English Scottish	French Ukraine	Hungary Italy	
Last half of 20th century 1950 ->	Chinese Korean	English Japanese	French Thai	East Indian Vietnamese	
Most recent 1980 ->	El Salvador Poland	Eritrea Somalia	Ethiopia Spain	Guatemala French	
Festivals in Winnipeg					

COMPREHENSION

Fill in the Blanks

Fill in the blanks below after listening to the talk. Use the information in your listening chart to help you. Some of these answers are tricky, so be careful. Listen as many times as necessary to find the answers. Use the words listed at the end of the exercise.

1. The _____ and the _____ have been in Manitoba for the longest time.

2. In the 1870s, English-speaking people came from _____.

3. By the 1890s, there was a large group of _____ immigrants.

4. By 1910, people from Ukraine, Hungary, and _____ had moved west too.

5. The farmers of _____ were the first to grow wheat.

6. During the last half of the 20th century, many immigrants came from _____.

7. The latest immigrants have come from _____ and _____.

Africa	First Nations peoples	Poland	Métis
Central America	Great Britain	Manitoba	Saskatchewan
East Asia	Icelandic	French	

There are two words that you did not use. Write a sentence for each of these words.

1. _____

2. _____

VOCABULARY EXPANSION

Synonyms

Part 1

Listen to the talk again. Listen carefully to find a synonym for each of the following words. You will hear the synonyms in the same order as the list on the next page.

The first one has been done for you.

1. remainder = _____rest_____

2. numerous = _____

3. create = _____

4. soil = _____

5. grow = _____

6. different = _____

7. celebrations = _____

8. Native peoples =_____

9. middle = _____

Part 2

Use one of the words in the left column above to fill in each blank below.

The groups of new immigrants were _____. Families came to settle in a new land where

the _____ was very _____ from what they were used to. This new country was

so strange that they felt they were in the _____ of nowhere. They had to learn to

_____ crops in new ways. At the end of their first growing season, they were satisfied

with their efforts and planned _____ before the cold winter arrived.

Word Forms

Fill in the following chart. You heard many of these word forms used in the talk.
The first one has been done for you.

Country	People	Language
England	English	English
	Irish	
	Scottish	
	French	
Sweden		
Denmark		
Norway		
Russia		
Poland		
Hungary		
Belgium		
Ukraine		
	Vietnamese	
	Thai	
	Japanese	
	Korean	
	Chinese	
Somalia		
Ethiopia		
Guatemala		

FOLLOW UP

Talking

Using your listening chart and your answers from the Comprehension section to help you, tell another group or class about the early immigrants to Manitoba.

Researching

Find out about the earliest immigrants in *your* province. Where did they come from? What did they do when they first arrived? What are the populations of immigrant groups in your province now? What problems do these immigrant groups face today?

Writing

In the last part of the talk, you heard about festivals that are held each year to celebrate the different cultures in Manitoba. Write about a festival that is important in your country of origin. Give the name of the celebration. Tell when it is held and why. Write about the food, the music, the games, and other events that happen during this festival.

Talking

Your teacher will ask you to make an oral presentation about your country. Bring maps, posters, pictures, clothing, and other articles to show your classmates about your heritage. If you have a classmate who is also from your country of origin, you might like to work with that person or in a small group.

Describing a Process

The following traditional recipes were brought to an ESL class by immigrants to Canada. The recipes might be similar to something from your country. Work in a small group. Read the recipes together and talk about how they are similar to, or different from, recipes in your culture. You might find these foods at the Farmer's Market in Winnipeg.

Russian Piroshkis
by Inna Nei

Ingredients for Filling	Ingredients for Dough
1 small cabbage, chopped	125 mL (1/2 cup) milk
1 medium onion, chopped	50 mL (1/4 cup) salted butter
50 mL (1/4 cup) oil	15 mL (1 tablespoon) dry yeast
salt and pepper to taste	50 mL (1/4 cup) warm water
1 hard-cooked egg	750 mL (3 cups) flour
	4 mL (3/4 teaspoon) salt
	50 mL (1/4 cup) sugar
	2 eggs, unbeaten

Make the filling:

1. Fry the cabbage and onion on medium heat in the oil until golden brown.

2. Add the salt and pepper and the minced hard-cooked egg and mix well.

3. Add the seasoning to your taste.

4. Set aside.

Make the dough:

1. Heat the milk and butter until the butter is melted.

2. Let the mixture stand until lukewarm.

3. Meanwhile, combine the water, sugar, and yeast in a warm bowl. Let this mixture stand until dissolved.

4. Add the milk mixture, the eggs, the salt, and half the flour.

5. Beat until mixed.

6. Continue adding the flour until it is all combined.

7. Turn the dough out on a floured board and knead until smooth. Work in more flour until the dough is no longer sticky.

8. Place the dough in a greased bowl and let it rise until it is doubled.

9. Punch it down and cut it into 18–20 pieces.

Continued on next page

Continued from previous page

10. Take one piece and spread it in your palm.

11. Put one tablespoon of filling in the centre, fold over and seal the edge.

12. Place the piroshkis, sealed side down, on a greased baking sheet.

13. Let them rise for 45 minutes.

14. Brush them with a mixture of an egg yolk and 2 tablespoons of water.

15. Bake at 200°C (400°F) for 25–35 minutes until they are golden brown.

16. Let them stand until warm and then serve.

Soor from Somalia
(Soup and accompaniment)
by Magda Sekaly

Ingredients for Soup

125 mL (1/2 cup) oil	1 potato
500 g (1 pound) of beef	5 mL (1 teaspoon) of salt
1 carrot	3 leaves of fresh basil
1 onion	2 mL (1/2 teaspoon) of cumin
4 cloves of garlic, finely chopped	2 mL (1/2 teaspoon) black pepper

Method

1. Chop the vegetables and garlic into small pieces.
2. Fry the chopped onion and garlic in the oil until they are golden brown.
3. Add the rest of the vegetables, the beef, and the seasonings.
4. Mix together and fry for a few minutes.
5. Add 1 cup of water.
6. Lower the heat and cook for 1 hour.

Ingredients for Accompaniment

500 mL (2 cups) of Cream of Wheat

1 small onion

2 cloves of garlic

25 mL (5 teaspoons) of oil

2 mL (1/2 teaspoon) of salt

Method

1. Chop the onion and the garlic very finely.
2. Heat the oil on the stove.
3. Fry the chopped onion until it is golden brown.
4. Add the chopped garlic, the salt, and the Cream of Wheat.
5. Mix well and add 500 mL (2 cups) of hot water.
6. Lower the heat and cover the pot.
7. Cook for 45 minutes.
8. Serve with the soup.
   Traditionally, it is eaten using the fingers.

Sprice (Lega Tepes) from Ethiopia
(a spicy meat sauce to eat with bread)
with personal comments
by Lulit Woldu

"We know this kind of food from a long time ago. It comes from small villages where there live little people. They are called lega tepes."

"This is all you have to do for your sprice sauce. Remember, this kind of stuff is good for you and it is easy to do it. Are you ready? Follow me. I'll show you how to do it easily."

Ingredients

1 onion, chopped

5 mL (1 teaspoon) of salt

2 cloves of garlic, finely chopped

125 mL (1/2 cup) of oil

250 g (1/2 pound) of meat

2 hot peppers

2 fresh tomatoes, chopped

Method

1. Chop the onion by hand. Put it into a bowl.
2. Add salt, oil, garlic, and fresh tomato. Mix well.
3. Cut the hot peppers into small pieces. Be careful, because they are hot.
4. Add the meat. Make sure you mix the ingredients together well.
5. Then fry in a pan for 10 minutes.
6. Eat this sauce with bread.

Fried Beans from Honduras

with personal comments by Rosalinda Arnoni

"This dish is very popular in Honduras. It's as common in Honduras as bread is at each meal in Canada."

Ingredients

500 g (1 pound) uncooked beans (pinto, turtle, or kidney)

3–4 cloves fresh garlic

1 medium onion, sliced

50 mL (4 tablespoons) of oil

1/2 medium onion, chopped

salt to taste

Method

1. Soak the beans for 2–3 hours in enough water to cover them.
2. Bring a large pot of water to a boil. Add the softened beans to the boiling water. Then reduce the heat to medium. Add the garlic and the sliced onion. Cover and stir from time to time.
3. When the beans are tender, put them in the food processor (without the broth) and mash them.

   "If you like, you can mash them with a fork — if you like to work hard."

4. Heat 50 mL (4 tablespoons) of oil in a frying pan. Add the chopped onion and fry until transparent. Add the puréed beans and fry them over low heat for 20–30 minutes. Add the bean broth a little at a time if it is needed, stirring constantly over medium-low heat until the beans are thick.

   "These beans are usually served as a side dish, eaten with tortillas and 'mantequilla' — a heavy cream similar to sour cream — or with cheese, fried plantain, rice, or any other typical Honduran dish."

Bring in a recipe from your country for one of the following:

i)   a stuffed pastry

ii) a soup

iii) a bread

iv) a vegetable dish

❖   Manitoba was the first province to give women the right to vote. This happened in 1916. Quebec was the last, in 1940. The federal government first allowed women to vote in federal elections in 1918.

Ontario

Listen to the Loon

• •

INTRODUCTION

Ontario has a diverse geography. There are grassy hills, rock outcrops, farmlands, marshes, forests, lakes, and rivers. All of these areas abound with wildlife. There are large and small mammals; fish, reptiles, and amphibians; and all sorts of birds. One of the most appealing birds is the loon. It is most familiar to everyone from the back of our one-dollar coin and twenty-dollar bill. What do you know about this bird? The talk in this section will give you some information.

VOCABULARY PREVIEW

Write the meanings of the following words. You may use a dictionary.

1. loon (noun) _____

2. beak (noun) _____

3. clumsy (adjective) _____

4. grasp (verb) _____

5. likeness (noun) _____

 ### SENTENCE CLUES

Listen carefully to the following sentences and fill in the blanks.

1. The common _____ is a black-and-white _____ that lives in Canada.

2. The robin held the worm in its sharp, yellow _____.

3. John was very _____, so he couldn't dance very well.

4. _____.

5. _____.

🔲 LISTENING TO THE TALK

The talk you will hear is about the common loon. You probably touch a likeness of this bird every day when handling money. The loon doesn't sing in the same way as most other birds. Its call is quite different. Listen and find out more about this beautiful bird.

The first time you hear the talk, just listen for the main ideas. As you listen for a second time, make notes using the following chart.

Listening Chart: Common Loons

Where they live	
What they look like	
How they move in water	
What they eat	
Where they spend the winter	
Where they spend the spring and summer	
The number of loons in Canada	

COMPREHENSION

True or False?

After you have listened to the talk, read the following sentences. Write the correct response (T for *True*, F for *False*, or N for *Not enough information*) in the blank at the beginning of each sentence. Use your listening chart to help you.

    T – *True*
    F – *False*
    N – *Not enough information*

_____   1. Loons live only in lakes.

_____   2. There are four different kinds of loons in the loon family.

_____   3. Loons are completely black, even their eyes.

_____   4. Baby loons look the same as the adults.

_____   5. Loons are as big as Canada geese.

_____   6. Loons are fast, efficient swimmers.

_____   7. Loons eat only fish.

_____   8. The loons' nest is neatly built, about 3 metres from the shore of a lake.

_____   9. Loons spend the winters in Mexico.

_____   10. Loons are good flyers, but must land on water.

_____   11. The loon is Ontario's provincial bird.

_____   12. Loons live all across Canada.

Now, rewrite the sentences you marked *F* to make them true.

_____

_____

_____

_____

_____

VOCABULARY EXPANSION

Antonyms

Part 1

Antonyms are words that have an opposite meaning. Listen for the antonyms of these words in the talk. The first one has been done for you.

1. murky ≠ <u>clear</u>

2. weak ≠ _____

3. clumsy ≠ _____

4. dull ≠ _____

5. neat ≠ _____

6. calm ≠ _____

7. scarcity ≠ _____

Part 2

Make up a sentence using each set of antonyms to compare two things. The first one has been done for you.

1. <u>Water in a swimming pool is clear, but water in a polluted river is murky.</u>

2. _____

3. _____

4. _____

5. _____

6. _____

7. _____

FOLLOW UP

Talking

Using your listening chart and the Comprehension section to help you, tell another group or class about the common loon.

Researching

i) From the talk, you know that there are four types of loons in the loon family. You heard about the common loon. Choose another loon, find information about it from a book in the library, and write a report about it.

ii) Find some information about the mating and parenting practices of the common loon. Write a report about these practices.

❖   Originally a pair of voyageurs in a canoe was supposed to be on the back of the one-dollar coin. Unfortunately, the mould got lost on the way to the mint in Winnipeg.

Mr. Bell's Inventions

· ·

INTRODUCTION

You probably use the telephone at least once
a day. Businesses use it a lot more often.
Telephones are used to talk to someone next
door, on the next street, in another city, or in
another country. Even computers use
telephones! Do you know who invented the
telephone? This talk will tell you about this
invention.

VOCABULARY PREVIEW

Write the meanings of the following words. Use a dictionary if you need one.

1. genius (noun) _____

2. deaf (adjective) _____

3. telegraph (noun) _____

4. lab (noun) _____

5. artificial (adjective) _____

6. distil (verb) _____

7. prosperous (adjective) _____

[🎞] SENTENCE CLUES

Listen carefully to the following sentences and fill in the blanks.

1. Albert Einstein was a mathematical _____.

2. A hearing aid is an _____ device to help a person who is partially _____.

3. Before the telephone, people sent quick messages by _____.

4. _____.

5. _____.

LISTENING TO THE TALK

You will hear a talk about Alexander Graham Bell. He invented the telephone. He also had many other ideas for new inventions. The first time you hear the talk, just listen for the main ideas. As you listen for a second time, make notes using the following chart as a guide.

Listening Chart: Mr. Bell's Inventions

	Where	**When**
Alexander Graham Bell was born		
He moved first		
		as a boy
He studied and worked		as an adult
He developed the idea for the telephone		while visiting his parents
His first voice experiment with the telephone happened		
His first telephone call in Canada happened		
Other inventions		
He died		

COMPREHENSION

Sentence Order

Put the following sentences in order by numbering them 1 through 8. They are about Alexander Graham Bell's life.

_____ He made his first American telephone call from Boston.

_____ He worked on many different experiments and inventions there.

_____ He worked in the United States as a teacher of people who are deaf.

_____ Alexander Graham Bell came to Canada as a boy with his parents.

_____ He made the first Canadian telephone call from his parents' home.

_____ He started thinking about a way to carry a voice across wires.

_____ He moved to Nova Scotia, Canada, because it reminded him of Scotland.

_____ He died at the age of 75 in his Nova Scotia home.

VOCABULARY EXPANSION

Antonyms

Part 1

Write the antonym of each of these words by using a prefix such as *in*, *un*, or *dis*.
The first one has been done for you.

1. correct ≠ <u>incorrect</u>

2. interested ≠ _____

3. proved ≠ _____

4. impressed ≠ _____

5. satisfied ≠ _____

6. continued ≠ _____

7. original ≠ _____

8. available ≠ _____

9. honour ≠ _____

Part 2

Now use one of the words to fill the blanks in these sentences.

1. Mr. Bell was _____ with just inventing the telephone.

2. He _____ working with deaf students after he moved to Canada.

3. The information that Mr. Bell was Canadian is _____.

4. Telephone service was _____ to many places at the time of Mr. Bell's death.

5. When he died, telephone service was _____ for one minute to _____ him.

FOLLOW UP

Talking

Using your listening chart and the answers to the Comprehension section to help you, tell another group or class about the invention of the telephone.

Researching

Do some research on some other forms of communication and their inventors.

- braille
- hearing aids
- transatlantic cable
- radio
- television
- sign language
- fax machines
- modems
- satellites

Writing

i) Pretend you were one of the people in the telegraph office when Mr. Bell made his third Canadian call. There was a party going on at his parents' house. Describe how you would feel hearing voices and music coming through a wire.

ii) Imagine you are Mrs. Bell. Write your diary entry for the day that your husband made the kite that lifted a man off the ground. What do you think *your* role would be?

❖ According to Stentor Communications, a 1994 survey found 16 261 044 telephone lines in Canada. These are network service lines. They do not count the multiple lines that go into businesses. This is quite a difference from Mr. Bell's single line!

A Thank-You Gift

INTRODUCTION

Since 1945, Holland has been sending tulip bulbs to Ottawa, Canada's capital city. The Dutch Royal Family sends thousands of bulbs every year. Each year, our capital city displays a show of colour more beautiful than the one the year before.

VOCABULARY PREVIEW

Write the meanings of the following words. Use a dictionary if you need one.

1. fled (verb 'to flee') _____

2. declare (verb) _____

3. exceptional (adjective) _____

4. perpetual (adjective) _____

5. display (verb) _____

SENTENCE CLUES

Listen carefully to the following sentences and fill in the blanks.

1. Refugees have _____ their countries for various reasons.

2. I think the Prime Minister should _____ a new national holiday on February 15th, Flag Day.

3. Wo Quan was _____.

4. _____

_____.

LISTENING TO THE TALK

Why does the Dutch Royal Family send so many bulbs to Ottawa every year? Listen to the talk and you'll hear the answer. Make notes on a separate piece of paper. You will be answering questions about what you hear.

▣ COMPREHENSION

Answering Questions

Answer the following questions after listening to the talk on the tape. Listen as many times as necessary to find the answers.

1. Why did the Dutch Royal Family flee to Canada?

_____

2. Where did they stay?

_____

3. What happy event occurred when the Royal Family was here?

_____

4. How did the Dutch Royal Family thank Canada for protecting them during the war?

_____

5. When is the Canadian Tulip Festival held in Ottawa?

_____

Listening for Numbers

Listen for the information you need to match the numbers below with the meanings on the right. The first one has been done for you.

_d_ 1. 50

____ 2. 20 000

____ 3. 10 000

____ 4. 200 000

____ 5. 3 000 000

a) the number of tulips that were blooming in Ottawa in 1951

b) the number of tulips that bloom now, to make Ottawa's Tulip Festival the largest in the world

c) the number of tulip bulbs Princess Juliana sent in 1946

d) the approximate number of years ago that the Dutch Royal Family came to stay in Ottawa

e) the number of tulip bulbs sent by the people of Holland right after the war

VOCABULARY EXPANSION

Word Forms

Part 1

The words in the chart below are from the talk. Fill in the chart with other forms of these words. The first line has been done for you.

Noun	Adjective	Verb	Adverb
protection	protective	protect	protectively
	delivery		- - - - -
	exceptional		
	perpetual		
collection			
		bloom	- - - - -
		organize	- - - - -
beauty			

Part 2

Now fill in the blanks below with words from your chart. It will be easier if you first decide which word form you need to use, then look in that form's column. Be careful of verb tense and agreement.

1. Hodan's mother put her arms around him _____.

2. Flowers of any kind _____ the environment.

3. The teacher will _____ the exams at the end of the period.

4. It must be very difficult to _____ the Tulip Festival!

5. In English, there is always an _____ to the rule.

6. I love to look at all the tulip _____.

WORD SEARCH

All the words in the list below are associated with the Tulip Festival. Find and circle the words in the puzzle. They may go across, up, down, diagonally, forwards, or backwards.

```
H O L L A N D S L A T E P H K
K G G S S G E U W R L M F S W
R R L S G V F A T P S N N K T
D S K X A R T K R D L E Y J Q
Z D W E U T M U N A D Q U V K
Y B L O O Y P A V R T L Q L K
H Q L T Z S S I A S I Y B T S
T O U Q X U T G H A V Y Y F L
C C L E O S H G N K T R A P H
N E T H E R L A N D S T E M C
V D T F C N G I P I W B F D S
S Y K B D T P W P P R W S I H
C A N A L T U L I P Y P J X G
Q N K D C U Y D V Z K Q S F H
Y E L L O W B C A P I T A L H
```

BULB	STEM
CANAL	PETALS
THOUSANDS	GARDEN
HOLLAND	PINK
COLOURFUL	JULIANA
YELLOW	DUTCH
SPRING	FESTIVAL
NETHERLANDS	RED
OTTAWA	TULIP
LEAVES	PURPLE
HAPPY	QUEEN
CAPITAL	MAY
GIFT	

FOLLOW UP

Talking

Using your notes and the answers to the Comprehension section to help you, tell another group or class about the Tulip Festival in Ottawa.

Describing a Process

The Life Cycle of a Tulip

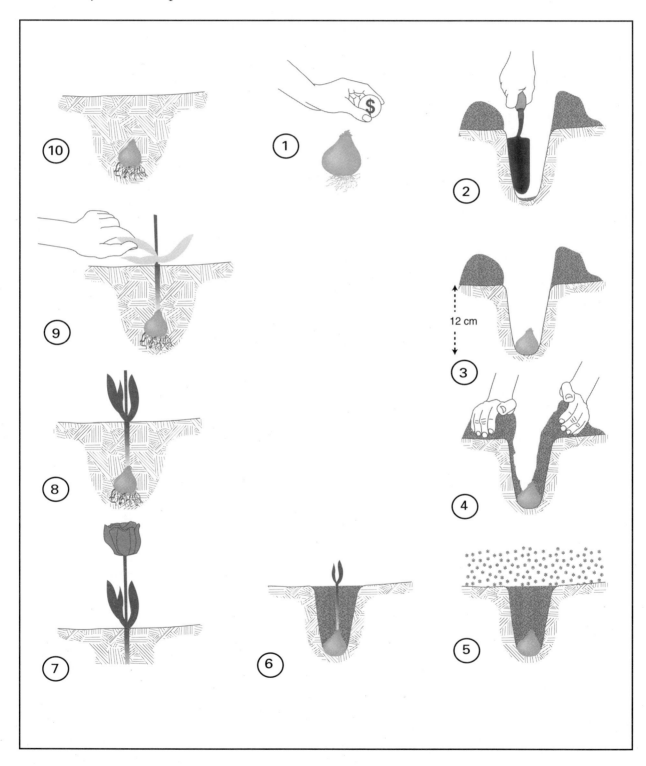

Look at the diagram on the previous page on the life cycle of a tulip. Now number the following sentences from 1 to 10 to match the information in the diagram.

_____ Dig a hole in your garden.

_____ The tulips bloom in many beautiful colours.

_____ Fill the hole with soil.

_____ The leaves turn yellow and die. Take them off the plant and throw them away.

_____ In the spring, the snow melts and the bulb begins to grow. It sends up green leaves.

_____ DON'T DIG UP THE BULBS!! Leave them in the ground and next spring you will have beautiful tulips again.

_____ The flowers die but the leaves stay green for two or three weeks longer. They are feeding the bulb with the sun's light. The roots are taking food from the soil. The bulbs begin to grow new baby bulbs (bulblets).

_____ Buy the tulip bulbs in the fall.

_____ The bulbs will sleep during the winter. The snow will cover the ground, but the bulbs will survive.

_____ Put one tulip bulb in each hole. The hole is about 12 centimetres deep.

In about five years, dig up the bulbs and separate the bulblets. Work the soil in the tulip bed. Plant all your old bulbs and new bulblets. Next spring, you will have more tulips!

Researching

Your teacher can help you find information about special festivals in your city or town. Or, call your local City Hall or Town Hall directly to find out if there is a special festival in your area. Write a short description about this festival.
- Why is it celebrated?
- Who puts it on?
- What activities are offered?
- When is it held?
- What makes it special for your town or city?

❖ Tulips originally came from Turkey. They were discovered there over 400 years ago by a man named deBusbucq. He brought some bulbs back to his home in Vienna and planted them in the royal garden. The story of how they spread across Europe is very interesting. Find out about it in your library.

Unit Six

Quebec

Our Tale of Two Cities
. . . .

INTRODUCTION

Quebec is one of Canada's oldest provinces. It joined Ontario, New Brunswick, and Nova Scotia to create the Dominion of Canada on July 1, 1867. Its first European settlers were the French, and its present culture reflects that history. French culture can be seen and felt throughout the province.

VOCABULARY PREVIEW

Write the meanings of the following words. Use a dictionary if you need one.

1. site (noun) _____

2. island (noun) _____

3. fur trader (noun phrase) _____

4. sophisticated (adjective)· _____

5. pavilion (noun) _____

6. cobblestoned (adjective) _____

SENTENCE CLUES

Listen carefully to the following sentences and fill in the blanks.

1. An _____ is an excellent _____ for a city.

2. The earliest French settlers were _____, with the help of the Native peoples.

3. Paris and London are very _____ European cities.

4. A World's Fair exhibits _____.

5. _____

_____.

LISTENING TO THE TALK

The province of Quebec includes two beautiful cities: Montreal and Quebec City. Both cities are located on the St. Lawrence River, the major water highway into the interior of Canada. Each has its own special character and special points of interest. Each city was important in Quebec's history and plays an important part in the province's present. Listen to find out about some of the interesting features of these two cities.

Listen to the talk on the tape twice. The first time you hear the tape, just listen for the main ideas. As you listen for a second time, make notes using the following chart to compare the cities.

Listening Chart: Our Tale of Two Cities

	Montreal	Quebec City
Location		
Physical Size		
Businesses and Workplaces		
Culture		
Festivals		
Historical notes		

██ COMPREHENSION

Scrambled Sentences

Unscramble the following sentences after listening to the talk on the tape. Use the notes in your listening chart to help you. Listen to the tape as many times as necessary to find the answers.

1. French-speaking Montreal city is in the world the second largest.

_____

2. the St. Lawrence River and the Ottawa River meet is Montreal located where on an island.

_____

3. a natural centre transportation was for early French explorers and The island fur traders.

_____

4. The 1967 1976 and the Summer Olympics were Montreal held in World's Fair.

_____

5. Quebec City is Quebec the capital Canada's of one of oldest cities.

_____

6. a large business and cultural role Quebec Montreal City has is smaller than but still.

_____

7. five major Quebec City There are in Montreal universities and.

_____

8. at the winter in Quebec City Winter Carnival Celebrate Quebec.

_____

VOCABULARY EXPANSION

Homonyms

Homonyms are words that sound the same but are spelled differently and have different meanings.

Part 1

Use the correct homonym to fill in the blank in each sentence.

1. The view from the top of Mount Royal was a beautiful _____. (sight, site)

2. When the ball began to _____ down the hill, the children ran after it. (role, roll)

3. The province of Quebec is proud of _____ French background. (it's, its)

4. Most Quebec businesses will not _____ anyone who cannot speak French. (hire, higher)

5. When you go _____ Montreal, you will hear French, and English _____.

   (too, two, to)

6. Shop owners in Quebec provide a service to more of _____ customers when they

   are able to speak both French and English _____. (their, there, they're)

Part 2

Now write a sentence for each homonym you did not use.

1. _____

2. _____

3. _____

4. _____

5. _____

6. _____

FOLLOW UP

Talking

Using the information in your listening chart and the Comprehension section to help you, tell another group or class about the province of Quebec.

Researching

Here is a list of important people from Montreal and Quebec City. Choose three of the people and do the following research:

• When were they born?

• When did they die?

• Why are they important to the history or culture of Quebec or Canada?

The library would be a good resource for finding the answers.

From Montreal:		From Quebec City:
Paul Bley	Claude Jutra	Marie-Claire Blais
Michel Brault	Oscar Peterson	Sylvie Bernier
Jehan Benoit	Maurice "Rocket" Richard	Marc Garneau
Geneviève Bujold	Mordecai Richler	Patrick Roy
Robert Charlebois	Michel Tremblay	
Leonard Cohen	Pierre Elliott Trudeau	
Marion Dewar	George Vanier	
Céline Dion	Caroline Waldo	
Jean Drapeau	Lucille Wheeler	
A.Y. Jackson		

❖ Many people in Quebec want to separate from Canada to make Quebec its own country. A referendum was held on October 30, 1995 and the people of Quebec voted for the province to remain within Canada. The vote was very close.

Unit Seven

New Brunswick

Fiddleheads

• •

INTRODUCTION

People all over the world love to eat. Some
people love hot, spicy dishes that 'burn' their lips,
tongue, and the passageway right down to their
stomachs. Others savour rich-tasting meats.
Some crave very sweet things. Yet others enjoy
fresh, juicy fruits or vegetables. There are many
different foods throughout the world. What
foods are your favourites?

VOCABULARY PREVIEW

Write the meanings of the following words. Use a dictionary if you need one to help you.

1. fiddlehead (noun) _____

_____

2. delicacy (noun) _____

3. tender (adjective) _____

4. fern (noun) _____

5. warning (noun) _____

6. patch (noun) _____

SENTENCE CLUES

Listen carefully to the following sentences and fill in the blanks.

1. Smoked salmon is a _____ served at special dinners.

2. The _____ young shoots will die in an early frost.

3. Tom had a small _____ of vegetables growing in the backyard.

4. _____?

5. _____!

54

🎞 LISTENING TO THE TALK

The talk you will hear is about fiddleheads. In this case, fiddleheads are not parts of an old ship or musical instrument, but a kind of food. Listen for a description of this fiddlehead, as well as where and when you can find it. Listen carefully because you will be answering questions about what you hear.

Listen to the talk twice. The first time you hear the talk, just listen for the main ideas. As you listen for a second time, make notes using the listening chart.

Listening Chart: Fiddleheads

When you can buy them fresh	
When you can buy them frozen	
Where you can buy them fresh	
Where you can buy them frozen	
Where you can find them fresh	
What they look like	
How you harvest them	
Warnings	1.
	2.

COMPREHENSION

Scrambled Sentences

Unscramble the following sentences. Write your good sentences on the long blanks below.

Next, put the sentences in a logical order according to the talk you heard by writing the numbers 1 through 6 on the short blank in front of each sentence.

1. to produce one spores or two plants for crop Leave next year's.
2. early the Fiddleheads in spring grow.
3. can many enjoy fiddleheads in different recipes You eating.
4. pick the that you Don't find all in a fiddleheads patch.
5. you you get to clean home When have them them well.
6. can in areas of New Brunswick, Quebec, find and You Ontario them damp.

_____ _____

_____ _____

_____ _____

_____ _____

_____ _____

_____ _____

VOCABULARY EXPANSION

Homonyms

Part 1

Choose the correct word to fill in each blank below. Many of these words are homonyms. Others are 'sound-similars' that are often mixed up.

1. Maple syrup and fiddleheads are _____ Canadian delicacies. (to, too, two)
2. Fresh fiddleheads are not _____ to buy. (cheap, cheep)
3. They like wet, _____ areas. (would, wooded)

4. This sprout is fairly easy to _____. (sea, see)

5. _____ you've found your patch, keep it a secret. (Ones, Once)

6. Use them within a _____. (weak, week)

7. As soon as it boils, _____ the water off. (pour, poor, pore)

Part 2

Now write a sentence using the words you did not choose. You will have to write two sentences for numbers 1 and 7.

1. _____

_____

2. _____

3. _____

4. _____

5. _____

6. _____

7. _____

_____

FOLLOW UP

Talking

Using the notes in your listening chart and the sentences in the Comprehension exercise, tell another group or class about fiddleheads.

Doing a Hands-On Activity

Here is a recipe for preparing fiddleheads. Perhaps your teacher can find some fiddleheads in the supermarket, or maybe you can go hunting for fiddleheads. If you have a kitchen in your school, you might be able to prepare this dish in class. Otherwise, find some fiddleheads at the local supermarket and try cooking them at home.

How to Cook Fresh Fiddleheads

1. Wash the fiddleheads in cold water. Be sure to remove all the brown, papery fluff from them.

2. Put the fiddleheads into a saucepan and cover them with cold, lightly salted water.

3. Cover the pan and bring the water to a boil.

4. As soon as the water boils, pour it off. You will see that the water has turned brown. Now cover the fiddleheads with more cold water and bring the water to a boil again. Pour off this second batch of boiling water.

5. Put cold water into the pot again. This time, bring the water to a boil, then turn it down and simmer for 10 to 15 minutes, or until the fiddleheads are tender, but not soft. Pour off the water.

6. Add salt, pepper, butter, and lemon juice and serve at once.

Researching

Find another recipe for fiddleheads.

Describing a Process

Bring in favourite recipes from your country that use fruits or vegetables not available in most Canadian supermarkets. Maybe you know of a special market where you can buy this fruit or vegetable, or maybe you grow it in your garden. Bring the fruit or vegetable to class and tell the other students about it. How does it grow in your country of origin? Is the imported product any different from the product you have in your country? Do you eat it raw or cooked? Is it expensive to buy in your country? Compare the price to what you paid here. Ask your teacher if your class can prepare some of your personal recipes.

❖ Ferns are among the oldest land plants. They appeared during the Devonian period, 395 to 350 million years ago. Some of them grew to be very large. They were the main food for plant-eating dinosaurs. By 300 million years ago, most of the plants on earth were ferns growing in tropical conditions. Now ferns grow in gardens and in the wild in all kinds of weather conditions. Ferns that serve as our house plants are usually tropical in origin.

High Tide

• •

INTRODUCTION

Canada has four provinces on the east coast that are affected by the tides of the Atlantic Ocean. Tides rise and fall all over the world, once or twice a day. Experts say that the tides in the Bay of Fundy between New Brunswick and Nova Scotia are the highest in the world! A tide like that can be like a monster if you are not prepared for the power it holds.

VOCABULARY PREVIEW

Write the meanings of the following words. Use a dictionary if you need one.

1. effect (noun) _____

2. affect (verb) _____

3. keel (noun) _____

4. float (verb) _____

5. dock (noun) _____

6. porpoise (noun) _____

7. erode (verb) _____

🎞 SENTENCE CLUES

Listen carefully to the following sentences and fill in the blanks.

1. The moon and the sun _____ the water in the seas.

2. The _____ of the moon and the sun on oceans is the tides.

3. A boat's _____ helps it to _____ evenly in the water.

4. Boats arrive at the _____ daily to take on supplies or passengers.

5. The _____.

6. The wind and the water _____.

LISTENING TO THE TALK

You will hear about the tides in the Bay of Fundy. Many tourists visit the area to watch the rising and falling tides. Listen to hear about this amazing act of nature.

Listen to the talk twice. The first time you hear the tape, just listen for the main ideas. As you listen for a second time, make notes using the following chart.

Listening Chart: High Tide

Where do tides happen?	
Why do tides happen?	
What moves when tides happen?	
Where are the highest tides in the world?	
As the tide floods in the Bay of Fundy, it passes the places listed in the left-hand column. Fill in the height of the tide at each place.	
Enters the Bay	No change
Grand Manan Island	
Cap d'Or Lighthouse	
Head of the Bay	
Cumberland Basin	
Nova Scotia's Minas Basin	

 COMPREHENSION

After listening to the talk on the tape, do the following exercise. Listen as many times as necessary to find the answers.

Scrambled Words

The sentences below contain some words that are scrambled. Unscramble the words and rewrite the sentences. The words that need to be changed are underlined in the first sentence.

1. When the trawe moves wtrados the ndla, we say the dite is foldingo.

_____

2. When the weart moves back to esa, we say the edit is bebing.

_____

3. The lpul of the nus and mono causes the sedit.

_____

4. Tides in the yaB of dFnuy are the shighet in the dorlw.

_____

5. Many sherfimen reaf the water at this mite.

_____

6. The water snode't get oto high in B.N.

_____

7. It's like a ditla vewa in a verri in N.S.

_____

8. It kames a wave wot remets high and vomes at 13 mk/h!

_____

VOCABULARY EXPANSION

Antonyms

Part 1

The following words are from the talk. For each one, write a word that means the opposite.

1. empty ≠ _____

2. rising ≠ _____

3. highest ≠ _____

4. close ≠ _____

5. later ≠ _____

6. incoming ≠ _____

Part 2

Use a word from the left-hand column on the previous page to fill in the blanks in the following sentences.

1. "I am expecting a letter in the _____ mail," said Mr. Braun.

2. "Where is Canada's _____ mountain?" asked Amal.

3. Daniel was sitting very _____ to his mother.

4. We must _____ the swimming pool to clean it.

5. Mohammed came at six o'clock and Khan arrived ten minutes _____.

6. The temperature was steadily _____ during the day.

Part 3

Now write a sentence of your own for each of the antonyms.

1. _____

2. _____

3. _____

4. _____

5. _____

6. _____

FOLLOW UP

Talking

Using your listening chart and your answers to the Comprehension section to help you, tell another group or class about the tides in the Bay of Fundy.

Researching

Animals of all kinds live in and around the Bay of Fundy. You can see humpback whales, porpoises, lobsters, and many types of fish. Sea birds flock to eat anything left when the tide has ebbed.

Choose a Bay of Fundy animal and write a report about it. Try to include information about its size, parenting habits, what it eats, and the environmental conditions it likes.

Writing

If you come from a country that borders the ocean, maybe you have seen the effects of tides. Write a story about tides you have seen. If you haven't seen any tidal effects, write about another interesting geographic occurrence you have seen.

❖ Tides flood and ebb at a different time every day, so sailors who are in areas affected by the tides must carry special tables or charts that help them calculate the times, heights, and distances of the tides. By doing these calculations, sailors protect themselves and their boats from harm.

Unit Eight

Nova Scotia

Follow the *Bluenose*

. . . .

INTRODUCTION

Have you ever wondered why there is a sailing ship on the back of our ten-cent coin? That ship was a famous sailing ship built in Lunenburg, Nova Scotia. It was christened *Bluenose*, and has gone down in Maritime history as a champion.

VOCABULARY PREVIEW

Write the meanings of the following words. Use a dictionary if you need one.

1. timber (noun) _____

2. mast (noun) _____

3. schooner (noun) _____

4. bow (noun) _____

5. eliminate (verb) _____

6. fortune (noun) _____

7. replica (noun) _____

SENTENCE CLUES

Listen carefully to the following sentences and fill in the blanks.

1. The type of _____ used in building fishing _____ was oak and birch found below the water line.

2. _____ were usually one tall tree trunk, straightened by force, trimmed, and sanded smooth.

3. The _____ of a tall ship cuts through the waves of the ocean.

4. Sailors wish for _____.

5. You can buy _____.

6. _____.

LISTENING TO THE TALK

As you listen to the talk, try to imagine a time when timber ships with billowing sails sped out to the fishing grounds on the Grand Banks, using only the power of the wind. What joy it would be for a captain to race his ship instead of just using it for working on the Grand Banks.

The first time you hear the talk, just listen for the main ideas. As you listen for a second time, make notes using the following chart.

Listening Chart: Follow the *Bluenose*

The *Bluenose*		
Birth - where		
- when		
- why		
Captain		
Races entered (years)	Elimination races to	International Fisherman's Race to
Challenger		
Date *Bluenose* left Canada		
Date of her death		

COMPREHENSION

After listening to the talk on the tape and using the information in your chart, do the following exercise. Listen as many times as necessary to find the answers.

Split Sentences

Find the correct ending for each of these sentence beginnings. Write out the complete sentences.

1. The *Bluenose* schooner was built _____

2. Angus Walters learned to sail _____

3. *Bluenose* was really built to race _____

4. Captain Walters and the *Bluenose* won most of the races _____

5. *Bluenose* was put on the back of our dime _____

6. *Bluenose* and her crew won their last race _____

7. Captain Walters had to sell his beautiful ship _____

8. *Bluenose* sank _____

a) in 1938.

b) in 1946 off the coast of Haiti.

c) on his father's fishing schooner.

d) in a shipyard in Lunenburg.

e) in 1942 to the West Indies Trading Company.

f) against the Americans.

g) in 1937.

h) in the 20s and 30s.

VOCABULARY EXPANSION

Idioms

The following idioms developed from the eras of ships and sailors at sea.

Idiom	Meaning
a) *to jump ship*	to leave a ship (or other enterprise) without permission
b) *to run a tight ship*	to be very strict with the rules

c) *to take the wind out of someone's sails*   to make someone feel less confident about himself or herself

d) *to ship out*   to leave

e) *shape up or ship out*   usually given as a warning to either behave yourself and obey the rules, or else leave

f) *when your ship comes in*   when you suddenly have a lot of money or you are successful after working hard at something

g) *in shipshape*   very neat and tidy with everything in its proper place

Now write the correct idioms in the following sentences. Be careful about verb tenses and pronoun agreement.

1. When Fernando lost the race, it really _____.

2. When Amal had everything _____ at her new apartment, she invited her mother to visit.

3. Mr. Ali _____ at his accounting office.

4. When the *Polar Star* reached Halifax harbour, ten sailors _____.

5. Mohammed works hard and he'll retire early if _____.

6. "Is everyone packed for the trip?" asked Miss Noseworthy. "Then let's _____."

7. After Pete was late for work for the fifth time and he was not properly dressed for the job, his boss told him to _____.

Verb Tenses

Choose past tense verb forms to fill in the blanks and create sentences that make sense. Many of your choices may be irregular verbs.

1. Smith and Rhuland Yard in Lunenburg _____ the *Bluenose*.

2. Captain Angus Walters _____ his ship well in all kinds of weather.

3. The *Bluenose* _____ many other fishing ships in preliminary races.

4. The *Bluenose* _____ the International Fisherman's Race three years in a row.

5. The sailors often _____ to fight storms and high winds while working at sea.

6. Canada _____ home the race trophy forever in 1938.

7. Canada _____ the *Bluenose* by putting her on the back of our dime.

8. When the *Bluenose* _____ to her death, many Canadians _____ sad.

Extra Challenge

Change the above sentences to the passive tense. The first one has been done for you. Some of these sentences are difficult. Think about the meaning of each before you write the passive form.

1. The *Bluenose* was built in the Smith and Rhuland Yard in Lunenburg. _____

_____

2. _____

_____

3. _____

_____

4. _____

_____

5. _____

_____

6. _____

_____

7. _____

_____

8. _____

_____

FOLLOW UP

Talking

Using your listening chart and your answers to the Comprehension section to help you, tell another group or class the story of the *Bluenose*.

Researching

Visit the library. See if you can find more information about the *Bluenose*. Look for answers to these questions:

- How big was it?
- What kind of wood was used to build it?
- What were the sails made of?
- How are the replica's sails different from the original sails?
- Who sails the replica of the *Bluenose*?

An alternative research project would be to compare and contrast old fishing schooners to modern-day fishing boats. How close are today's methods to those of 50 or 60 years ago?

Writing

Imagine you are a member of the crew of the *Bluenose*. This is the scene.

"The sky was a brilliant blue and a few clouds raced across the sky. Slowly, darker clouds started to build on the horizon. The wind started to blow harder. We had all the sails set. Suddenly…"

Finish writing this adventure story.

❖ There was another famous Nova Scotian ship called the *Marie Celeste*. It was built and launched in 1861. Then on December 5th, 1872, it was found drifting on the Atlantic with all its cargo on board, but not a trace of the crew! What do you think might have happened?

Unit Nine

Prince Edward Island

Red Lobster

. . . .

INTRODUCTION

Although Prince Edward Island is Canada's smallest province, it is popular for many reasons. In 1867, the Fathers of Confederation met in Charlottetown, the capital city, to make Canada a country. P.E.I. was also the home of author Lucy Maud Montgomery, creator of the famous red-haired girl, Anne of Green Gables. Today, P.E.I. is the centre of lobster fishing in the Maritime provinces. What a lot of fame for such a small island!

VOCABULARY PREVIEW

Write the meanings of the following words. Use a dictionary if you need one.

1. inshore (adjective) _____

2. mainstay (noun) _____

3. species (noun) _____

4. pound (noun) _____

5. tradition (noun) _____

6. decline (noun) _____

SENTENCE CLUES

Listen carefully to the following sentences and fill in the blanks.

1. Most fishermen in P.E.I. use _____ fishing boats.

2. Fishing and farming are the _____ of the island's economy.

3. The dogcatcher brings all stray dogs and cats _____.

4. _____ from generation to generation.

5. _____.

70

🎞 LISTENING TO THE TALK

Prince Edward Island is sometimes called a northern island paradise. There are warm summers and beautiful, sandy beaches. There is fresh ocean air. There is a variety of seafood available all year long. But the king of seafood is the Prince Edward Island lobster. Listen and learn more about this shellfish and other ocean delicacies.

The first time you hear the talk, just listen for the main ideas. As you listen for a second time, make notes using the following chart.

Listening Chart: Red Lobster

What does the number mean?	
54 million kg	
$53 million	
5060	
2500	
19 kg	
2400	

What happens to the lobsters that are caught?		
Many	Some	Smaller ones
Other shellfish	Winter jobs of fishermen in P.E.I	

COMPREHENSION

True or False?

Part 1

After you have listened to the talk, read the following sentences. Write the correct response in the blank at the beginning of each sentence. Use the listening chart you filled out to help you.

T – *True*

F – *False*

N – *Not enough information*

_____   1. Prince Edward Island is Canada's smallest province.

_____   2. P.E.I. fishermen produce 54 million pounds of fish and shellfish each year.

_____   3. Half the people in the province are employed by the fishing industry.

_____   4. The American lobster is also a Canadian lobster.

_____   5. Many lobsters that are caught are immediately exported.

_____   6. Smaller lobsters are thrown back into the sea to get bigger.

_____   7. Prince Edward Island is famous for its lobster festivals.

_____   8. Other festivals focus on different types of shellfish and fish.

_____   9. *Aquaculture* is the art of taking the salt out of sea water.

_____   10. Some kinds of lobsters are green and some are red.

_____   11. Fishermen even fish during the winter months.

_____   12. The fishing industry in the Maritime provinces is in trouble.

Part 2

Now, rewrite the sentences you marked *F* to make them true.

_____

_____

_____

_____

_____

_____

OPINIONS

Discuss the following questions.

1. Why do you think the American lobster is the only species of lobster that can live in Canada?
2. Why might certain kinds of shellfish be raised at special fish farms?
3. Why do you think the fishing industry is declining on the east coast of Canada?

VOCABULARY EXPANSION

Synonyms

Synonyms are words that have either the same meaning as, or a very similar meaning to, other words.

Part 1

The words in Column A below are words you heard in the talk. Match these words with a synonym from Column B.

Column A	Column B
1. collect = _____	commerce
2. exported = _____	average
3. industry = _____	harbour
4. plunged = _____	sold overseas
5. port = _____	citizens
6. reasonable = _____	lowered
7. residents = _____	hot
8. spicy = _____	get

Part 2

Choose one word or phrase from Column B to fill in the following blanks.

The fishermen _____ their lobster traps into the cold water around the island. Later

ships sailed into the _____ and unloaded their lobster traps before heading out again.

The _____ size of a lobster was about 1.5 kilograms. Many of the lobsters were quickly loaded into large cases to be _____.

The _____ of many P.E.I. towns enjoy the summer season, during which they can entertain the many tourists who come for the lobster festivals. Visitors enjoy dipping lobster into melted butter or _____ sauce. Delicious!

FOLLOW UP

Talking

Using your listening chart and the answers to your Comprehension section to help you, tell another group or class about lobster fishing in P.E.I.

Researching

i) Canada has many different kinds of natural resources. Choose one from the following list.
   • fish
   • oil
   • natural gas
   • forests (timber)
   • minerals — gold, nickel, copper, silver
   • hydro-electric power

Do some research to find out which province (or provinces) is famous for this resource. How many people does the industry employ? What items are produced with this natural resource?

ii) Canadian farms produce many products. These products vary from province to province, depending on the climate and the geography. Choose one product from the following list.
   • beef
   • dairy products
   • peaches and pears
   • apples
   • potatoes
   • green vegetables
   • wheat and wheat products

Find out which province (or provinces) is famous for this product. How many people does the industry employ?

❖   The most profitable vegetable crop in Canada is the potato. A large percentage of Canada's total potato output springs from the rich, sandy soil of P.E.I.

❖   Fresh potatoes contain 78 percent water and 18 percent starch. About 75 percent of the dry weight of a potato is carbohydrate.

❖   Potato starch is used in the manufacture of alcohol, as well as adhesives such as glue and paste.

Unit Ten

Newfoundland

Newest Province, Oldest History

. . . .

INTRODUCTION

Newfoundland is Canada's tenth province. It is made up of two parts: the island of Newfoundland off the far northeast coast of Canada, and Labrador, which is on the mainland. Newfoundland is part of the Canadian Shield and Appalachian landform regions. The last glaciers scraped most of its rock clean of deep topsoil. People sometimes call it "The Rock." On March 31, 1949, it became the last province to join Canada.

VOCABULARY PREVIEW

Write the meanings of the following words. Use a dictionary if you need one.

1. archaeological (adjective) _____

2. Scandinavia (noun) _____

3. Norse (adjective) _____

4. sod (noun) _____

 ## SENTENCE CLUES

Listen carefully to the following sentences and fill in the blanks.

1. There have been some interesting _____ discoveries in Newfoundland.

2. The _____ are people who come from _____.

3. _____.

🖭 LISTENING TO THE TALK

Recent archaeological discoveries have proven that the first Europeans visited the land that is now Canada almost 2000 years ago. However, Native peoples were living there long before that. Listen to the talk to learn about some of Canada's Native peoples and the first European settlers.

The first time you hear the talk, just listen for the main ideas. As you listen for a second time, make notes using the following chart.

Listening Chart: Newest Province, Oldest History

When	Who	Other Information
	Innu - 1. Montagnais 2. Naskapi	
2500 years ago		
	Inuit	
1000 years ago		
500 years ago		
	Vikings	

COMPREHENSION

Fill in the Blanks

After listening to the talk on the tape and using your listening chart to help you, fill in the blanks below with the correct words. Listen as many times as necessary to find the answers. Choose the words from the box below the sentences. The first blank has been filled in for you.

1. The first people to settle in the eastern area of Newfoundland were the <u>Innu</u>.
2. The _____ people of this group lived in the forests.
3. The Naskapi hunted for caribou, seals, and _____.
4. These early Innu spoke _____.
5. The Dorset hunted sea _____.
6. The Scandinavian people came to the island and probably met these _____ Natives.
7. Later, the _____ replaced the Dorset group.
8. The _____ helped European settlers who arrived in the 1500s.
9. The early Inuit taught the _____ about northern mammals and helped establish the fur trade.
10. L'Anse aux Meadows is the site of an early _____ settlement.

Dorset	Europeans	Innu	Inuit	Inuktitut
mammals	Montagnais	polar bears	Viking	Micmacs

VOCABULARY EXPANSION

Passive Verb Practice

Rewrite the first eight sentences in the above exercise using the passive tense. The first one has been done for you.

1. The eastern area of Newfoundland <u>was first settled</u> by the Innu.
2. _____
3. _____
4. _____
5. _____
6. _____
7. _____
8. _____

Pronoun Relationships

In long passages, pronouns and demonstrative adjectives are often used to refer to a previous word or words.

Example:

Early explorers who came from Europe were looking for a short route to East Asia. They never found it because it doesn't exist south of the Arctic Ocean. When they touched land, they were in North America. They didn't find the shortcut, but they did find fish — thousands of them. Never before had fishermen seen so many fish in one place! They could just throw baskets over the side of the ship and pull them up full.

In the following passage, the pronouns, demonstrative adjectives, and possessive adjectives have been circled. Draw a box around the noun or noun phrase they refer to. Then draw an arrow from the circle to the box.

Another Native group that lived on the island were the Beothuk. They lived on the northeastern and southern coasts. Some historians believe that these were the Natives the Vikings first met when they came west from Greenland. The Beothuk painted their faces red with a red dye, probably ochre, for certain ceremonies. Maybe this was the reason the North American Natives were called "redskins" by some Europeans. The Beothuk lived in tents covered with animal skins, and they hunted with bows and arrows.

Little by little, European settlers on the island pushed the Beothuk groups farther into the interior. Many of them escaped across the water to Labrador. There, their civilization began a slow decline. Many died through starvation or diseases brought by the Europeans. The last known survivor, a young woman named *Shawnandithet*, died in 1829. Before she died, she told her captors of the suffering of her people.

FOLLOW UP

Talking

Using your listening chart and the information in this unit to help you, tell another group or class about the Native groups and early Europeans in Newfoundland.

Researching

Newfoundland's history is a fascinating one. Choose one of the following topics to research:

- Guglielmo Marconi's experiment with long-distance communication: The path to the radio.
- Joining the Dominion of Canada: Was it the right choice?
- The challenges for today's Maritime fishing industry.

Writing

Choose one of the following topics.

i) Imagine you are a Native person when the first Vikings arrive. Describe what you see, how you feel, and how you react to these new people coming to your land.

ii) Imagine you are a new immigrant who arrived in 1605. What do you see on the land and in the water? How do you feel when you see this rocky, forested land? How do you feel when you encounter the Native peoples who don't speak your language?

Time Line

Write the names of the peoples in the blanks above or below the correct date on this time line.

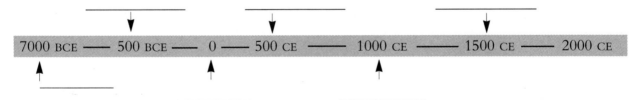

7000 BCE ——— 500 BCE ——— 0 ——— 500 CE ——— 1000 CE ——— 1500 CE ——— 2000 CE

NOTE: The abbreviations BCE (Before Common Era) and CE (Common Era) are now often used in place of the traditional abbreviations BC and AD.

DID YOU KNOW?

❖ Argentia, in Newfoundland, is the foggiest place in Canada. It has fog an average of 256 days each year.

The Yukon

Yukon Gold

INTRODUCTION

The Yukon in Canada's North was not the warmest place for immigrants to be in the late 1800s, but it did have one attraction — gold! Brave, adventurous people searched this cold land, hoping to find a fortune. A few of them returned home rich. Most left disappointed. Others stayed and made the Yukon their new home.

VOCABULARY PREVIEW

Write the meanings of the following words. Use a dictionary if you need one.

1. plateau (noun) _____

2. tributary (noun) _____

3. prospector (noun) _____

4. to stake a claim (verb phrase) _____

5. to strike it rich (verb phrase) _____

SENTENCE CLUES

Listen carefully to the following sentences and fill in the blanks.

1. The Yukon has mountains, rivers, and large _____.

2. Dawson Creek is a _____ of the Klondike River.

3. Every _____ had a single goal — _____.

4. _____.

LISTENING TO THE TALK

Gold was discovered in the Yukon in the late 1800s. Many people lost their life-savings trying to find the gold. A few lost their lives. Listen to the talk and you'll learn about that crazy time about 100 years ago in Canada's history.

The first time you hear the talk, just listen for the main ideas. As you listen for a second time, make notes using the following chart.

Listening Chart: Yukon Gold

The Yukon		
Location		
Land formations		
Names of some rivers and creeks		
Weather and temperatures	Winter	Summer
Gold was discovered!		
When		
Where		
By whom		
Prospectors came from these places		
What this time in Canadian history is called		

COMPREHENSION

Scrambled Sentences

The following sentences are a paraphrase of the story you heard on the tape, except that the words in each sentence are all mixed up. Also, the sentences are arranged in the wrong order.

First, unscramble the words to make a complete sentence. Remember, a sentence begins with a capital letter, so use that clue to help you. Then put a number in front of each sentence to place them in the correct order.

The first and last sentences have been done for you.

a) in On Rabbit Creek 1896, August 17, gold was discovered.

b) were Most of the Americans people.

c) a tip because Robert Henderson of by a Canadian prospector named it He found.

d) searched for Millions of gold dollars were by people spent who.

e) lies The Yukon Territory northwest corner in the of Canada.

f) prospectors succeeded in becoming Unfortunately, very few rich.

g) came Rich people gold to find and poor from the north south.

h) discovered by an George Washington Carmack, and his brothers-in-law It was American, Native.

i) the It is Klondike Gold Rush remembered for historically best.

j) was claimed every metre of that creek and other waterways in the Klondike area Soon.

a) _____ _____

b) _____ _____

c) _____ _____

_____

d) _____ _____

e) __1__   The Yukon Territory lies in the northwest corner of Canada.

f) __10__   Unfortunately, very few prospectors succeeded in becoming rich.

g) _____ _____

h) _____ _____

i) _____ _____

j) _____ _____

VOCABULARY EXPANSION

Compound Words

Part 1

Match a word from Column A with a word in Column B below to make a compound word from the story.

Column A	**Column B**
1. snow_____	light
2. north_____	night
3. day_____	one
4. every_____	where
5. over_____	west
6. water_____	made
7. steam_____	boat
8. hand_____	fall
9. any_____	way

Part 2

Now use a compound word from above to fill in each blank in the following sentences.

1. Many items were _____ during the early days in Canada.

2. Some gold seekers became rich _____.

3. Gold was found in the _____ part of Canada.

4. _____ was asked to bring a favourite book to school.

5. You can't find gold just _____ in Canada.

6. Transportation on the water was by _____ 100 years ago.

7. There is heavy _____ in some parts of Canada.

8. The Klondike River is a Yukon _____.

9. The sun shines brightly during _____ hours.

Word Forms

Part 1

The words in the chart below are words you heard in the talk. Fill in the chart with other forms of these words.

Noun	Adjective	Adverb
jealousy		
	northern	
		geographically
history		
	strong	
		hopefully

Part 2

From the chart above, choose one word for each of the following sentences.

The sentences below appear in the same order as the lines of words above. The first one has been filled in for you.

1. a) The location of the gold mine was his <u>jealously</u> guarded secret.

    b) _____ can sometimes turn good friends into enemies.

2. a) The _____ location kept a lot of people away.

    b) Winter winds were blowing from the _____.

3. a) Some people are interested in studying the _____ of the North.

    b) _____ speaking, the Yukon is in the northwest corner of Canada.

4. a) The Yukon is interesting geographically and _____.

b) If you visit Dawson City, you can see some _____ buildings.

5. a) Great _____ was required to climb the mountains.

    b) The police _____ suspected the murderer was the young prospector who had

      just arrived.

6. a) Prospectors searched _____ for gold.

    b) Unfortunately, many people's _____ disappeared.

FOLLOW UP

Talking

Using your listening chart and your answers to the Comprehension exercise to help you, tell
another group or class about the Klondike Gold Rush.

Researching

Choose one of the two topics described below and do research to find the answers to the
questions.

i) Find out about other gold mines in Canada.
    • Where are they?
    • How is the gold actually mined?
    • What is done to extract the gold?
    • What is the gold used for?

ii) Do you know about another Yukon 'gold' that has nothing to do with the valuable mineral
    found in the Yukon? As a matter of fact, this gold is found on the east coast of Canada too.
    • What is it?
    • How much is produced?
    • How is it used?

Writing

Imagine you are a prospector. Write about your success in finding gold — or your disappointment
in finding nothing.

Literature About the North

There are many stories and poems about the people and places of the Klondike Gold Rush. Some of this poetry was created by Robert Service. He was an immigrant from England who spent a lot of time in Canada's North, particularly the Yukon. One of his famous poems tells about an American prospector who found a way to get warm in the cold of the North. Here is the first verse.

The Cremation of Sam McGee

There are strange things done
in the midnight sun
By the men who moil for gold;
The Arctic trails have their secret tales
That would make your blood run cold;
The Northern Lights
have seen queer sights
But the queerest they ever did see
Was that night on the marge of Lake Labarge
I cremated Sam McGee.

Another poem by Robert Service tells about a dishonest prospector, Dan McGrew, who stole gold from another. Here is the first verse.

The Shooting of Dan McGrew

A bunch of the boys were whooping it up
in the Malamute saloon;
The kid that handles the music-box was hitting
a jag-time tune;
Back of the bar, in a solo game,
sat Dangerous Dan McGrew,
And watching his luck was his light-o'-love,
the lady that's known as Lou.

❖ The highest mountain in North America is located in the Yukon. Mount Logan, which is very close to the western border of the territory, is 5951 metres high.

Unit Twelve

The Northwest Territories

The Beauty of the North

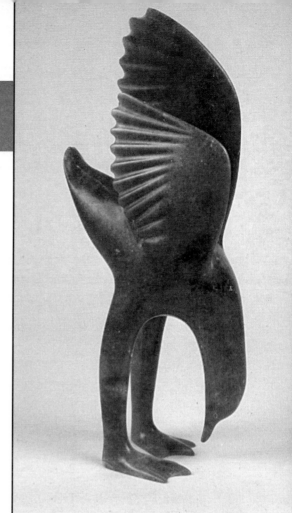

INTRODUCTION

Welcome to the North! The Northwest Territories cover 3 million square kilometres, which is about one-third of all of Canada's land mass. The Territories stretch from the northern borders of B.C., the Prairie provinces, and James Bay, all the way up to the North Pole. From east to west, they cover four time zones, yet the population is one of the smallest in Canada. You might think it is an inhospitable place, but if you go there you will likely find a land that begs you to return.

VOCABULARY PREVIEW

Write the meanings of the following words. Use a dictionary if you need one.

1. iceberg (noun) _____

2. wildlife (noun) _____

3. roam (verb) _____

4. sculptors (noun) _____

5. soapstone (noun) _____

6. appliquéd (adjective) _____

 ### SENTENCE CLUES

Listen carefully to the following sentences and fill in the blanks.

1. Huge _____ can be as tall as a multi-story apartment building.

2. The _____ of Canada is probably quite different from the wildlife in your country of origin.

3. Herds of caribou _____ the plains of the North.

4. _____ to carve beautiful symbols of their culture.

5. _____.

🎞 LISTENING TO THE TALK

The Native peoples of the North are divided into three basic groups: the Inuit and the Inuvialuit who live above the tree line; the Dene who live mainly in the forests and river valleys; and the Métis, the descendants of Native peoples and early European settlers. The lives of these people are very different from those of the people who live in the south.

Listen to the talk to find out how one aspect of the Native peoples' culture—art—reflects this cultural difference in a beautiful way.

The first time you hear the talk, just listen for the main ideas. As you listen for a second time, make notes using the following chart.

Listening Chart: The Beauty of the North

Geography	
Wildlife	1. southwestern 2. on vast eastern plains 3. in oceans and seas 4. northeastern
Basic groups of people in the North	1. 2 3. 4.
Where people sell their art	1. 2. 3.

Cape Dorset art	1.
	2.
Baker Lake art	
Taloyoak art	
Fort Providence art	
Fort Laird art	

 COMPREHENSION

Use your listening chart to help you do the following exercise. Listen as many times as necessary to find the answers.

Split Sentences

Part 1

Read each of the 10 sentence endings below. Then match each ending with one of the sentence beginnings. Write the ending on the line following each beginning.

Endings

a) are adding new materials to their traditional art.

b) are at home in the northeastern part.

c) makes money from selling art.

d) create beautifully appliquéd wall hangings.

e) is a famous printmaker.

f) cover the land and water most of the year.

g) believe that their art keeps their culture alive.

h) make up 60 percent of the population.

i) roam in the southwestern part of the Territories.

j) carve soapstone into shapes of animals and images of themselves.

Beginnings

1. Ice and lots of snow _____.

2. Dall's sheep, black bears, and grizzly bears _____.

3. Polar bears, musk-ox, and arctic fox _____.

4. Native peoples _____.

5. A high percentage of the Native population _____

_____.

6. The Inuit _____.

7. The Dene _____.

8. Kenojuak _____.

9. Today's Native artists _____.

10. The elders in Native groups _____.

Part 2

Now make up questions that would give each of the above answers.

1. _____

2. _____

3. _____

4. _____

5. _____

6. _____

7. _____

8. _____

9. _____

10. _____

VOCABULARY EXPANSION

Homonyms

Homonyms are words that sound similar but are spelled differently and have different meanings. Below, choose the correct homonym for each sentence and fill in the blanks. You may have to change the homonym slightly to make the sentences grammatically correct.

1. A cold wind _____ all night.
2. The bright, _____ sky was reflected in the cold, still water.
   (blue, blew)

3. Many animals live in the _____ of the North.
4. The baby laughs whenever he _____ the little doll.
5. The old hunter _____ the harpoon and kills the seal.
   (sees, seas, seize)

6. A king _____ until his death.
7. It hardly ever _____ in the Northwest Territories.
8. A horse is guided by wise use of the _____.
   (rains, reins, reigns)

9. The capital of the Northwest Territories is on the shore of _____ Slave Lake.
10. You build a fire on a _____ in your fireplace.
    (great, grate)

11. In many places in the North, groceries are delivered by _____.
12. Musk-ox and caribou roam the _____ of the North.
    (planes, plains)

13. Did you know that _____ are mammals?
14. Sometimes you can hear the _____ of wolves on a long, cold night.
    (wails, whales)

15. Your _____ skin will freeze quickly in the below zero temperatures on Baffin Island.
16. Polar _____ are the most dangerous when they are hungry.
    (bare, bear)

FOLLOW UP

Talking

Using your listening chart and the other exercises to help you, tell another group or class about the North.

Researching

i) This talk has outlined the art of the northern peoples. Find more detailed information about some of the art of these peoples. For example, some Inuit are talented in other arts, such as singing, dancing, and acting.

ii) The southern part of Canada has inspired many artists as well. Here is a list of a few of them. Find out why these artists are important.

- The Group of Seven
- Yousuf Karsh
- Jack Bush
- Toller Cranston
- Karen Kain

- Margaret Atwood
- Stephen Leacock
- Robertson Davies
- Mario Bernardi
- Glenn Gould

Making a Picture

Draw or paint a picture that shows something about your life in Canada or how you feel living in Canada. Then draw or paint a picture of something that shows the culture of your original country.

❖   Seven-eighths of an iceberg's mass is below the water. People thought the *Titanic,* a famous cruise ship, was unsinkable. On its first voyage in 1912, it hit an iceberg off the coast of Newfoundland and sank to the bottom of the sea. Many passengers were killed.

Unit Thirteen

Nunavut

Our Newest Territory

INTRODUCTION

NEWS BULLETIN — April 1, 1999

Iqaluit, Nunavut - After years of negotiation, Nunavut is Canada's newest territory. Celebrations are planned here in the capital city and in community halls all over the territory.

ᖃᐅᔨᓴᕐᓂᖅ

ᑐᓵᕐᓴᐅᑎᒃ - ᐊᐱᕆ 1, 1999
ᐃᖃᓗᐃᑦ, ᓄᓇᕗᑦ - ᐊᕐᕌᒍᓂ ᐊᒥᓲᓂ ᐊᖏᖃᑎᒌᒋᐊᕐᓚᕐᑎᓪᓘᓐᓂ ᓄᓇᕗᑦ ᑲᓇᑕᒧᑦ ᐃᓕᕐᒋᐊᑕᐅᓴᓐᓇᓕᕐᐳᖅ. ᖅᐃᐊᐱᐊᕐᓂᐅᑎᑦ ᐊᓛᑕᐅᓯᒃᐱᐊᐳᐃᓴᐊᑦᒍᑦ ᑕᕝᕙᓂ ᓄᓇᕐᐱᐊᑐᓐᓂᐊᐅᑦ ᐊᒻᒪᓗ ᓄᓇᕐᕋ ᐱᓐᒍᑎᕐᐱᓐᕋ ᓄᓇᕗᑦᒥᒥ.

VOCABULARY PREVIEW

Write the meanings of the following words. Use a dictionary if you need one.

1. Inuktitut (noun) _____.

2. referendum (noun) _____.

3. legislation (noun) _____.

4. allocate (verb) _____.

5. democratic (adjective) _____.

6. legislature (noun) _____.

SENTENCE CLUES

Listen carefully to the following sentences and fill in the blanks.

1. _____ is a written language of symbols.

2. A _____ is a right of people living in a _____.

3. The_____ passed _____ to _____ more money to the new territory of Nunavut.

4. _____.

LISTENING TO THE TALK

At the beginning of this unit, you read a news bulletin about the creation of Nunavut, Canada's newest territory.

Now you will be hearing the transcript of the complete newspaper article. The first time you hear the talk, just listen for the main ideas. As you listen for a second time, make notes using the following chart.

Listening Chart: Nunavut—Our Newest Territory

Date of birth	
Area	Description Square kilometres
Area belonging to the Inuit	Square kilometres
Native rights	1. 2. 3.
Type of government	
Population	Total Percentage Native
Location of capital city	

COMPREHENSION

True or False?

Part 1

After you have listened to the talk, read the following sentences. Write the correct response in the blank at the beginning of each sentence. Use your listening chart to help you.

T - *True*

F - *False*

N - *Not enough information*

_____ 1. Nunavut is in the eastern part of the Arctic.

_____ 2. Nunavut joined Canada in 1905.

_____ 3. Nunavut covers almost one-third of Canada's land mass.

_____ 4. Half of Nunavut is governed by the Inuit.

_____ 5. One way the federal government is helping the territory is through financial contributions.

_____ 6. Inuit can fish for salmon, tuna, northern sharks, and seals.

_____ 7. There are more Native peoples living in Nunavut than non-Natives.

_____ 8. The capital city is Yellowknife.

_____ 9. A lot of people from southern Canada will take over most of the jobs in the territory in the next 50 years.

_____ 10. Beautiful flowers bloom in the Arctic during the short summer.

Part 2

Rewrite any sentences that you marked false to make them true.

_____

_____

_____

_____

VOCABULARY EXPANSION

Antonyms

Part 1

Below are words from the talk. Write a word that means the opposite of each of the following words.

1. agreement ≠ _____

2. approved ≠ _____

3. eastern ≠ _____

4. whole ≠ _____

5. total ≠ _____

6. created ≠ _____

7. succeed ≠ _____

8. equality ≠ _____

9. northern ≠ _____

10. warm ≠ _____

Part 2

In the following paragraph:

- Separate the words into good sentences. Use a capital letter at the beginning of each sentence and a period at the end.
- Use a capital for nouns where it is required.
- Use one of the vocabulary words from the exercise above to fill in the blanks.

canada was _____ over 125 years ago. all provinces and territories did not join at that time only _____ provinces formed the new dominion of canada in the next ten years the _____ provinces and _____ territories joined the young country the last province, newfoundland, entered confederation in 1949 then there was a _____ of ten provinces and two territories late in the 20th century, two major things happened first the province of quebec tried to leave canada, but failed to do so by a very narrow margin in a referendum vote canada as we know it was not _____ secondly legislation was _____ in parliament and a new territory was _____ nunavut covers the _____ part of the canadian arctic everyone hopes that the new territory does not _____ in its endeavour

FOLLOW UP

Talking

Using your listening chart and the answers to the Comprehension section to help you, tell another group or class about Canada's newest territory, Nunavut.

Researching

1. Find out about new businesses in Nunavut.
2. Find out about education, jobs and training, arts, and family units in some communities of Nunavut.
3. Find out details about Nunavut's weather and environment.

Writing

If you wanted to visit the new capital city of Iqaluit, how would you get there? Call a travel agent to find out about types of available transportation, timetables of service, and cost, as well as about types of accommodation (hotels, motels, etc.) in the capital. What tourist activities are available once you get there?

Write an article to encourage people to visit the capital city and other areas of Nunavut.

Interviewing

Have you had the opportunity to get to know any Native Canadians? If so, ask one person how he or she feels about the new territory. Write his or her response in a paragraph format and present it to the class.

If you do not know any Native Canadians, interview a classmate to find out his or her feelings about the new territory and report to the class.

❖ The Inuit have their own television station. They produce many different kinds of programs. The most popular one for children is about a cartoon character named Super Shamou, who is an Inuit Superman!

Unit Fourteen

Canada

It's a Big Country!

INTRODUCTION

Geographically, Canada is the second largest country in the world. It stretches from the Atlantic Ocean to the Pacific Ocean and from the North Pole to the U.S. border. There is a lot of space here, but most of it will never be settled because the geography will not allow it. Immigrants come from every country to find a new life here. We welcome them and try to help them make their dreams come true.

VOCABULARY PREVIEW

Write the meanings of the following words. Use a dictionary if you need one.

1. 49th parallel (noun phrase) _____.
2. vast (adjective) _____.
3. zone (noun) _____.
4. varied (adjective) _____.
5. extend (verb) _____.
6. descendants (noun) _____.

SENTENCE CLUES

Listen carefully to the following sentences and fill in the blanks.

The border between Canada and the United States is close to the _____. Canada's area is _____; its land _____ from sea to sea. Its _____ geographic _____ will surprise and delight anyone who comes here. You and your _____ can enjoy a good life in Canada.

📼 LISTENING TO THE TALK

You will be hearing about Canada as a whole: its size, its geography, and its people. Canada has so much to offer. What part of Canada do you like best?

The first time you hear the talk, just listen for the main ideas. As you listen for a second time, make notes using the following chart.

Listening Chart: Canada — It's a Big Country!

Size	Total area East to west North to south
Longest highway	Name Length
Time zones	How many? Names of zones
Geographic features	1. 2. 3. 4. 5. 6. 7.
People	Canada's population Province with the largest population Province with the smallest population

COMPREHENSION

True or False?

Part 1

After you have listened to the talk, read the following sentences. Write the correct response in the blank at the beginning of each sentence. Use your listening chart to help you.

T – *True*

F – *False*

N – *Not enough information*

_____   1. Canada is the largest country in the world.

_____   2. There are high mountains in Nova Scotia.

_____   3. Farmers in Canada grow peaches, pears, and apples.

_____   4. Other farmers raise dairy and beef cattle.

_____   5. British Columbia is on the west coast.

_____   6. St. John's is the capital city of New Brunswick.

_____   7. Saskatchewan has four seasons.

_____   8. It is always cold in the far north.

_____   9. You can travel across Canada in a train.

_____   10. The train travels beside the Trans-Canada Highway.

_____   11. The Trans-Canada Highway starts in St. John's and ends in Vancouver.

_____   12. In the far north, the sun never sets in the winter.

_____   13. The Rocky Mountains are in Alberta and B.C.

_____   14. Some parts of Canada will probably never be settled.

Part 2

Now, rewrite the sentences you marked *F* to make them true.

_____

_____

_____

_____

_____

VOCABULARY EXPANSION

Comparatives and Superlatives

Part 1

Fill in the chart below with the comparative and superlative adjectives. The first one has been done for you.

Adjective	Comparative	Superlative
big	bigger	biggest
small		
old		
new		
high		
low		
hot		
cold		
warm		
cool		
far		
close		
long		
short		
sunny		
cloudy		

Part 2

When making comparisons, you use the phrase ". . . -er than. . . ."

When making a superlative statement, you use the phrase "the. . .-est."

Ask a question using one of the adjectives from the chart to give you the following short answers. The first one has been done for you.

1. <u>What is the name of the longest paved highway in the world?</u>

    The Trans–Canada Highway.

2. _____

    Saskatchewan.

3. _____

    Prince Edward Island.

4. _____

    The Rocky Mountains.

5. _____

    Quebec.

6. _____ smaller than _____

    Yes, it is.

7. _____ colder than _____

    No, it isn't.

8. _____ is bigger than _____

    The Northwest Territories.

9. _____ is warmer than _____

    British Columbia.

10. _____ are closest to _____

    Ontario and Saskatchewan.

Now answer these questions.

1. Which province has the largest population?

   _____.

2. Which province has the warmest winters?

   _____.

3. Which territory is farthest west?

   _____.

4. Which province is the smallest?

   _____.

5. Where are the oldest hills?

   _____.

6. Which province is the farthest east?

   _____.

7. Which province is closest to the middle of Canada?

   _____.

8. Which province has winter weather warmer than Manitoba's?

   _____.

9. Which is colder in the summer, southern Saskatchewan or northern Quebec?

   _____.

10. Which province has the smaller population, Alberta or Nova Scotia?

   _____.

FOLLOW UP

Writing

Choose one of the following subjects and write a short paragraph:

- Why is Canada important to you?
- Compare your original country to Canada. Consider size, population, geography, and weather.

Labelling a Diagram

Look at the map of Canada. Fill in the names of each province and territory. Then find the time zones pictured in the front of your local telephone book. Draw these time zones on your map.

Filling Out a Table

Time Zones

When it's	in	it's	in
seven o'clock	St. John's		Victoria.
	Toronto	4:30 p.m.	Edmonton.
three o'clock	Winnipeg		Quebec City.
	Yellowknife	midnight	Halifax.
noon hour	Fredericton		Regina.
	Charlottetown	7:00 a.m.	Whitehorse.
2:30 p.m.	Ottawa		Vancouver.
	Ottawa	6:00 p.m.	my city.
now	my city or town;		Ottawa.

Interviewing

Find someone who was born in Canada. Ask him or her the question, "Why is Canada important to you?" Then report your findings to the class.

Reviewing

Match the following headlines with the correct date on the time line. Write the appropriate letter in the box directly above or below the date. The headlines review events covered in earlier units of the book. Look back at your listening charts and Comprehension exercises if you need to.

a) A New Territory is Created
b) Alexander Graham Bell Makes Telephone Call in Ontario
c) Banff National Park Created
d) *Bluenose* Honoured on Canada's Dime
e) *Bluenose* Launched in Lunenburg
f) Dominion of Canada is Born
g) Gold is Found in the Klondike
h) Land Available at One Dollar an Acre
i) Newfoundland Joins Canada
j) Summer Olympics in Montreal
k) Princess Juliana Sends a Thank-You Gift to Canada
l) Ukrainians, Poles, and Hungarians Immigrate to Manitoba

□	□	□	□	□	□
1876	1885	1910	1937	1949	1999

1867	1881	1896	1921	1946	1976
□	□	□	□	□	□

❖ Ten thousand years ago, Canada was covered with a layer of ice 3 kilometres thick.

Bibliography

· ·

Bodsworth, Fred. *The Pacific Coast — The Illustrated Natural History of Canada*. Toronto: Natural Science of Canada Limited, 1970.

The Canadian Encyclopedia — Second edition. "Crustacean Resources," Volume I, p. 549; "Klondike Goldrush," Volume II, pp. 1143–44; "Lobsters," p. 1235. Edmonton: Hurtig Publishers, 1988.

Colombo, John Robert. *1001 Questions about Canada*. Toronto: Doubleday Canada, 1986.

Hancock, Lyn. *Northwest Territories*. Discover Canada series. Toronto: Grolier Limited, 1993.

Hornby, A.S., ed. *Oxford Advanced Learner's Dictionary*. Oxford: Oxford University Press, 1989.

Josephson, Judith Pinkerton. *The Loon*. Mankats, MN: Crestwood House, 1988.

Kessler, Deirdre. *Prince Edward Island*. Discover Canada series. Toronto: Grolier Limited, 1992.

LeVert, Suzanne. *Newfoundland*. Let's Discover Canada series. New York: Chelsea House Publishers, 1992.

_____. *Prince Edward Island*. Let's Discover Canada series. New York: Chelsea House Publishers, 1991.

Martin, Sandra. *Quizzing Canada*. Toronto: Dundurn Press Limited, 1987.

Mitchell, Dorothy. "Bluenose." Seamanship Publication Committee. *Porthole*. March 1994.

_____. "Bluenose, Part II." Seamanship Publication Committee. *Porthole*. June 1995.

Payne, Elizabeth. "Loon Now Official Symbol." Queen's Park Bureau, *The Ottawa Citizen,* June 25, 1994.

Rayburn, Alan. *Naming Canada*. Toronto: University of Toronto Press Inc, 1994.

Stevenson, Marylee. *Canada's National Parks — A Visitor's Guide*. Scarborough, ON: Prentice-Hall Canada Inc., 1991.

Thurston, Harry. *Tidal Life — A Natural History of the Bay of Fundy*. North York, ON: Camden House Publishing, 1990.

Warren, Helen, ed. *Oxford Learner's Dictionary of English Idioms*. Oxford: Oxford University Press, 1994.

Wehmeier, Sally, ed. *Oxford Wordpower Dictionary*. Oxford: Oxford University Press, 1993.

White, Marion Frances. *Newfoundland and Labrador*. Discover Canada series. Toronto: Grolier Limited, 1994.

Photo Credits